BEAUCHAMP
walter   tailors
est.   1908
TORONTO

Nigel,
Hope you enjoy the history.
Aug 11, 2021
Thanks for your support of friendship
over the years.
All The Best,
Tony B.

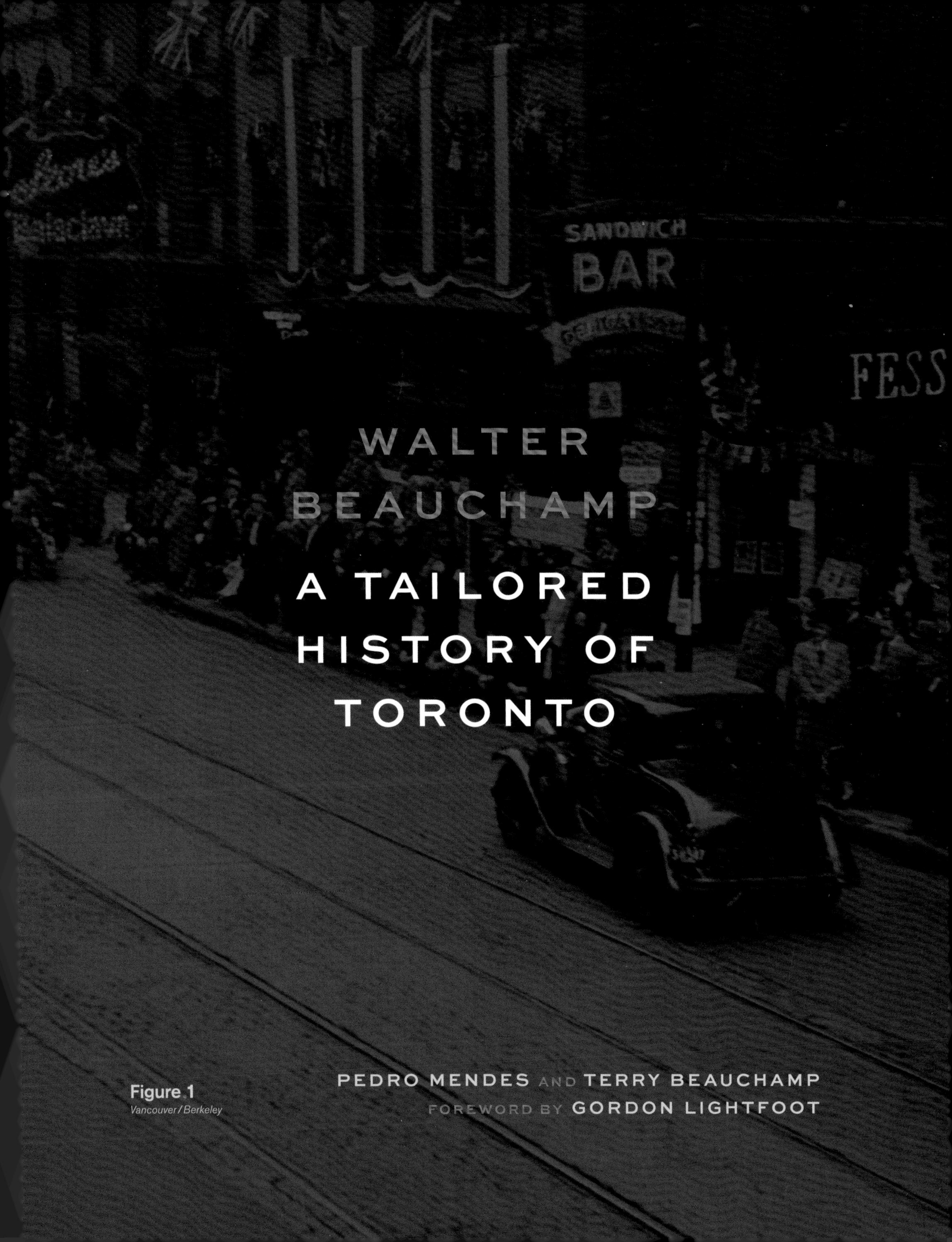

WALTER
BEAUCHAMP

A TAILORED
HISTORY OF
TORONTO

Figure.1
Vancouver / Berkeley

PEDRO MENDES AND TERRY BEAUCHAMP
FOREWORD BY GORDON LIGHTFOOT

ON THE COVER *A detail of the Royal Flying Corps' "maternity" tunic ordered from Beauchamp & How by J.B. Fitzgerald on August 17, 1917.*

PAGE i *Walter Beauchamp Tailors redesigned its logo in 2008 to celebrate its 100th anniversary. The new logo features the swan-and-crown badge used by the Beauchamp Earls of Warwick in the Middle Ages.*

PAGES ii–iii *Tailors' Row dressed up for the royal visit of King George VI and Queen Elizabeth in the spring of 1939. Although the future location of Beauchamp & How can be seen at 77 King West (the Score's Balaclava sign), the company was at 91 King, to the right of the camera lens, when this photograph was taken.*

17 18 19 20 21   5 4 3 2 1

Cataloguing data available from Library and Archives Canada
ISBN 978-1-927958-89-6 (hbk.)

Design by Natalie Olsen
Author photographs by Lawrence Cortez (top), Kathryn Palmateer (bottom)
Editing by Sarah Brohman
Copy editing by Marilyn Thomson
Proofreading by Melanie Little
Indexing by Jane Broderick
Front cover photograph by Lawrence Cortez
Printed and bound in China by C&C Offset Printing Co., Ltd.
Distributed in the U.S. by Publishers Group West

Figure 1 Publishing Inc.
Vancouver BC Canada
www.figure1publishing.com

*This book is dedicated
to the memories of
Bruce Beauchamp and
Chief Warrant Officer
Scott F. Patterson of the
Queen's Own Rifles
of Canada.*

CONTENTS

When I first entered Walter Beauchamp Tailors in 2003, I had no idea I was becoming a part of history. I needed a wardrobe for a comeback tour and I knew I could count on Terry, Alfonso, Mary, and everyone else at Beauchamp's to take care of it expertly. They have made me various items over the years, many of which I wear on tour and on stage. The more time I spent with Terry, however, the more I heard about his family's uncommon history. Come to think of it, that's probably why we hit it off so well: Terry is part tailor, part storyteller. Sometimes I even wondered whether Terry's extraordinary stories about his father and grandfather, not to mention the legions of customers who shopped at Beauchamp's, were too good to be true. Turns out, these customers were all real and sometimes even more remarkable than Terry realized. I am so happy for Terry that the history of Beauchamp's is now revealed in the book you are holding.

But this book is much more than the history of an excellent tailor. It rolls out the fabric of our shared history and tells the story of Toronto, and of Canada, from the vantage point of the Beauchamp shop windows. It's a story that stretches back to before the Great War and into the lives and struggles of generations of Canadians who have served in our Armed Forces. And, of course, it's a story that takes us into the boardrooms and living rooms of those who helped make Toronto the city that it is today. And that is what's so special about this book: the tailor's perspective. As I can attest, a relationship with a tailor is an intimate one. Sometimes you feel closer to your tailor than to your doctor or your priest. Although, I can assure you, tailor-client confidentiality is sacred— right, Terry?

What I like most about this book is the personal stories it contains. You will read about the people who wore the clothes Beauchamp's made and their riveting adventures. They are soldiers who fought at the Battle of Vimy Ridge in the First World War,

D-Day colonels and their men who served in the Second World War, once-notable but now-forgotten figures from the early twentieth century and latter-day celebrities of various kinds, as well as prime ministers, mayors and judges, authors, explorers, and inventors, young and old, men and women. What weaves them together is not only a wardrobe tailored by three generations of Beauchamps, but also their compelling stories that offer us rare glimpses of our city and our country.

My life's work is telling stories, Canadian stories at that, so I feel a deep connection to this book and the stories it tells. I like to tell stories about things that really happened, to me and to others. I believe we can learn most about life and ourselves from the stories of others and the stories of our own that we share with others. We can learn a lot from this book, not just about tailoring or Canada's history, but also about the human spirit.

GORDON LIGHTFOOT
SEPTEMBER 2016

A NOTE ABOUT NAMES

Two important names in this book need clarification: "Walter" and "Beauchamp." We shall begin with the latter.

Upon entering the shop for the first time, many customers ask to speak with "Mr. Bo-SHAW." Such customers are instructed, politely and patiently, by a staff member—who has done so countless times—that the name is pronounced "BEE-chum." The Beauchamp family was originally French, but settled in England during the Norman Conquest in the eleventh century. Like most French surnames in England, Beauchamp became anglicized over time. The family remained in England until the mid-1800s, when the founder's grandfather Richard moved to Canada, where Walter's father George was born. The pronunciation of the Beauchamp name is the most obvious clue that a customer is brand new to the shop. (Adding to this confusion, in the 2000s Terry persuaded a family-owned art gallery based in Quebec City to open an outlet in the premises adjoining his store.

The name? Beauchamp Art Gallery, with the family's surname pronounced *à la française*.) Officially the company was known as Beauchamp & How before 1969; it has been Walter Beauchamp Tailors ever since. But customers have always simply called the shop Beauchamp's.

Several "Walters" appear in this book: the founder Walter Beauchamp, his son Walter Beauchamp, and the third-generation owner, also named Walter Beauchamp. The family has never used a suffix, such as "the Second" or "Junior," to differentiate the Walters. The second Walter Beauchamp was called Sonny by his family and friends. And the third Walter Beauchamp has been called Terry (the *ter* in Walter) all his life. Indeed, as a young boy he was scarcely aware that his given name was not actually Terry. For the sake of simplicity, this book refers to the shop's founder as Walter Beauchamp Sr., to his son as Walter Beauchamp Jr., and to the current owner as Terry Beauchamp.

INTRODUCTION

The history of most tailors is preserved in their paperwork: not their business receipts and invoices, but the measurement ledgers and paper patterns they create for each customer. In the ledgers are recorded the intimate details of each body, including the exact measurements of the belly, the shoulders, and even the seat—measurements that are sometimes hidden from customers to shield them from uncomfortable truths. Tailors also note any oddities, such as slouched shoulders, an overerect posture, or unequal leg lengths. Cumulative ledgers show how a body ages and, as the notes become more personal and idiosyncratic, how the relationship between tailor and customer evolves.

Once a customer dies, it makes little sense for tailors to retain such records. After all, they will never be used again. Yet some of the storied houses of Savile Row in London—an old city with a deep belief in the value of the past—have kept such tailoring records for centuries. Unfortunately, like many businesses, Walter Beauchamp Tailors has discarded much of its history. And likewise, through the years, Toronto, where the company makes its home, has demolished buildings and razed neighbourhoods, sacrificing much of its rare architecture of historical significance. Only in recent decades have preservationists' voices begun to be heard.

With a limited amount of archival material from the company to draw upon, the authors have had to reconstruct the history of Walter Beauchamp from other sources. We have delved deep into city archives and military museums, pored over decades of newspaper stories, and conducted dozens of interviews with individuals whose memories stretch back as far as the 1930s. In the process, we have uncovered not only the story of Beauchamp's, but also a history of Toronto, as seen through the eyes of a tailor.

The Founding of Beauchamp & How

Walter Beauchamp Sr. didn't set out to become a tailor. In fact, on December 22, 1906, almost two years before he opened his shop in Toronto, he was facing death in the shadow of the Pinos Altos Mountains in New Mexico. For several months, Walter had been working as a cattle rancher in the small outpost of Fort Bayard. The work was hard and unforgiving, so to get some respite he and two other ranchers had spent a good part of the day drinking and gambling in Silver City. The two-hour horse ride back to Fort Bayard took them along winding mountain trails as the sun was going down over the Pinos Altos.

The other ranchers rode ahead, followed by Walter. Behind them a heavy cold-storage wagon drawn by four horses was lumbering along the steeply undulating path. The driver had drunk a bit too much "nose paint" in the city, and just as the wagon reached a summit on the trail he nodded off. He was so intoxicated that he continued sleeping as he toppled from the wagon into the sand and bushes by the side of the trail. His horses, knowing they were heading home and sensing their driver was gone, started to pick up speed.

Ahead in the twilight, Walter had no idea the wagon was barrelling along without a driver. He leaned back in the saddle as his group started down a steep hill into a narrow valley. That's when he heard the wagon coming up fast behind them. He glanced back, only to see that the driver was gone and that, with the weight of the heavy wagon behind them, the horses were advancing at deadly speed.

Walter and his men spurred their horses into a gallop. They rushed toward the bottom of the hill, knowing that if the wagon reached them, travelling at full speed on the narrow path, no one would survive. Walter saw that the trail immediately headed steeply upward again. Could he and his men make it to the incline before the runaway wagon caught up with them?

They rode at top speed down the slope. Walter could hear the panicked breathing of the wagon's horses right behind him. But, as they started up the next hill, the weight of the wagon began to tire the horses. Walter jumped from his saddle. The wagon had slowed enough that he could climb on and bring it to a halt.

What was he doing, Walter wondered, two thousand miles from his hometown? His family and friends in Toronto were preparing to celebrate Christmas on a frigid December day while he sat sweating in the New Mexico heat, feeling his adrenaline ease away. If truth be told, this son of a prominent Toronto hotelier, working day and night as a ranch hand, was there to escape. Back in Toronto, people assumed he had fled the city because his young wife, Bessie (née Giles), had died of septicemia in the summer and he was heartbroken. Little did they know that, even before his wife died, Walter had fallen for someone else. His new love was a mere teenager, the niece of a prominent business leader to boot. If anyone learned that he was not wearing mourning clothes but instead was writing weekly love letters to a sweetheart, neither he nor the young lady would live down the scandal.

The young woman Walter had fallen for, with whom he had secretly held hands

that summer as they strolled alongside the Beaver River near Meaford, Ontario, was Viola Mackenzie, daughter of Alexander and niece of William. William Mackenzie was soon to be knighted for helping connect the country with his Canadian Northern Railway and for linking various areas of Toronto with the Toronto Railway Company. Walter was a graduate of tony Upper Canada College and came from a family of successful businessmen, but Viola was practically Canadian aristocracy. She would have brought disrepute to the Mackenzie family if their courtship had come to light.

In February of 1907, Viola embarked on a ten-month journey to Europe with her sisters and William Mackenzie. During her trip, she received letter after letter from Walt, as she called him in her diary, though none of the envelopes bore the sender's name or return address. She kept the letters detailing the secret affair to herself. She even hid the photo Walt sent of himself decked out as a cowboy atop his horse in New Mexico. And, though she admitted to flirtations with other boys in England and Scotland in her diary, none were serious.

In his letters to her in Europe through-out 1907, Walter assured Viola he was living a righteous life, albeit indulging in a bit of gambling while trying to stay off the drink. He made the occasional flirtatious comment, such as how pretty she looked in the photo she had sent him, or how he had found a bunch of mistletoe and wished she were around so he could steal a kiss. Mostly he recounted the daily exploits of working the land in New Mexico. But, as the months wore on, Walter wrote more about plans for his return home.

Above all, he was in need of a new suit. He asked his friend Alf How to order one from tailor Frank Burton at 73 King Street West because "no one [else] can make anything I like half so well." Walter also took care to order a suit made with a lightweight fabric, knowing it would please Viola. Second, Walter was eager to get back into business. Before fleeing Toronto, he had owned a hotel, like his father. But Walter wanted to go into the rapidly growing clothing industry, Toronto's biggest employer at the time. He hoped to become the local agent for the Regal Shoe Company of England if he could find a storefront on Yonge Street, the city's up-and-coming shopping district.

The rise of Yonge Street was but one aspect of the boom Toronto was experiencing when Walter returned home in July of 1907. As the city annexed the surrounding neighbourhoods and received an influx of immigrants from overseas and workers from the rest of the country, its population reached nearly 350,000 by the end of 1910—an increase of more than 80 percent since the turn of the century. Toronto ranked second only to Montreal as the economic powerhouse of the nation. It was the ideal time to go into business.

But the idea of being a shoe salesman was short lived. Walter had been friends with Alfred "Alf" Deans How since they were teenagers. They had often gotten into mischief in Beaverton, Ontario, where their families had nearby cottages. Instead of a shoe business, Alf had another career idea for Walter. Alf had been working as a junior cutter at Frank Burton's tailoring shop since 1900 and was ready to go out on his own. But he didn't have the capital to start a business. Alf's father worked at the *Globe* as a typesetter, a respectable position that paid a decent salary. But, unlike Walter's family, the How family's pockets weren't deep enough to set Alf up in business. So he made Walter a proposition.

Next to Frank's shop in an attached space at 73½ King Street West was O'Brien's Limited, a women's tailoring company that did piecework. Alf knew the space could accommodate a second small business. Why not open a tailoring shop of their own? They'd start modestly, with Alf doing all the cutting, and bring in jobbers (temporary tailors) as needed. With Walter's business acumen—and his connections to Toronto's wealthy elite— Alf knew they could succeed. Alf recognized that it was Walter's money that would make the business happen, so even though Walter wasn't a tailor, Alf proposed they name the company Beauchamp & How.

Walter's sweetheart, Viola, may well have thought King Street was a fortuitous location, for her father Alexander had been born just steps away. When her grandfather,

John Mackenzie, came to Canada from Scotland in the 1830s, he had settled his family on a small strip of farmland around King and Bay Streets. "But he was too far from the water," Viola recalled in 1973, "so a few years later they packed up and moved to Kirkfield." Six decades later, her future husband would start his own business on that former farmland.

Despite Yonge Street's rise to prominence, King Street West was a promising place to launch a venture in 1908. In the Toronto of the late nineteenth century, King between York and Bay was *the* street to see and to be seen on. One of the first thoroughfares in the city to be paved, it allowed carriages and coaches to let off their well-born passengers in style, for elsewhere the city was still deserving of the nickname Muddy York. The street was lined with high-end saloons, merchants, and men's clothiers, such as tailors R. Score & Son, as well as Edward Dack's shoe company. Dack's would eventually become a household name, remaining in the same place until the strip was demolished in 1962 (see page 89).

This section of King Street was known as Opera Lane because patrons in white

tie would stroll along it and through an archway next to 77 King (the future address of Beauchamp & How) to reach Theatre Lane, a narrow street that ran parallel to King behind the row of shops. Eager to be surrounded by such grandeur and so many other tailors, Walter and Alf not surprisingly jumped at the opportunity to launch their business there, even in a modest shop. In October of 1908, Beauchamp & How was incorporated, and Walter and Alf set about establishing their business.

The company's early advertisements and letterhead did not list its full address— perhaps Walter and Alf sensed their lowly status on King Street. Instead of the cumbersome 73½ King Street West, Walter adopted the term Tailors' Row. No one else used "Tailors' Row" in advertising, even though a disproportionate number of tailors could be found on the south side of the street between the

Moorish Palace Hotel at 55 King (and Bay) and the Imperial Bank at 139 King (and York). In fact, of the forty-five or so businesses, twenty were tailors. Other tailors may have used the term colloquially, but Walter's appropriation of it was an early indication of his business savvy. In one fell swoop he not only obscured the company's humble address, but he also elevated the King Street strip where it was located, making it sound like a place nestled between London's Savile Row and Jermyn Street.

Unlike the tailors on those venerable London streets, though, Beauchamp & How advertised its wares. England's tailors, especially the fine houses of Savile Row, regarded advertising as tawdry and unseemly, relying instead on word of mouth and personal recommendations. Though deeply conservative in matters social and religious, Toronto's citizens welcomed new business tactics wholeheartedly. Every tailor took out ads in the *Daily Star*, the *Globe*, the *Mail and Empire*, the *Toronto Evening Telegram*, and other broadsheets. Establishing what would become a Beauchamp tradition, the company kicked off an audacious marketing plan, though the term "marketing" was not used at that time. To distance themselves from the older, more established tailors on the row, Walter and Alf used a modern-sounding slogan in their early years: "Tailors to Young Men." They knew that older men were set in their sartorial ways and had already acquired their wardrobes, which were meagre by today's standards, comprising perhaps two or three suits and one piece of formal wear. Young men were also more likely to trust a tailor who was open to Edwardian styles and trends, instead of sticking to the Victorian fashions of their fathers' generation.

Tailors to Young Men
ONE PRICE ONLY $24.00

TELEPHONE MAIN 6644
CABLE ADDRESS: BEAUCHAMP, TORONTO

Beauchamp & How
Limited

TAILORS' ROW
KING STREET WEST,
TORONTO,

June 5/09

Dear Via

I'm going to play a joke
on you by writing to you
two days in succession
haven't really any thing
new to tell you, only
have a few minutes to
spare and thought I
would use them to good
advantage by writing
to you. Mrs Trehotty

R. SCORE & SON, LIMITED
TAILORS & HABERDASHERS
TORONTO

PREVIOUS *A letter from Walter Beauchamp Sr. to Viola Mackenzie, June 6, 1909, written on Beauchamp & How's original letterhead. The address was given as Tailors' Row, and the letterhead also featured the store's first advertising slogan, "Tailors to Young Men," and the company's competitive price of twenty-four dollars for all suits and overcoats.*

ABOVE *The cover of the R. Score & Son catalogue, 1911.*

FACING LEFT *A Beauchamp & How advertisement that ran in the* Toronto Daily Star *on October 9, 1908.*

FACING RIGHT *A Beauchamp & How advertisement that ran in the* Toronto Daily Star *on October 27, 1909.*

Walter and Alf had another trick up their sleeves: they advertised all their garments at the single price of twenty-four dollars, equivalent to about five hundred dollars today. This distinctive pricing strategy may seem a bit odd until you consider that over at 77 King was R. Score & Son, a company that eclipsed every tailor for blocks around. Established in 1842, this pre-eminent tailor occupied more than three thousand square feet and employed about sixty cutters, tailors, pressers, and salesmen. And it sold its suits for twenty-five dollars. Decades later, Walter and Alf's company would not only take over R. Score & Son's location, but would also acquire its customers and its prominence in Toronto's tailoring industry (see page 83). But all that was in the future.

In early *Toronto Daily Star* advertisements, Beauchamp & How's suits were proclaimed to be of high quality at low cost. But how did this "high-class custom tailor" offer "a properly tailored suit or overcoat at a reasonable price" despite having a cutter who was "one of the highest-salaried men in Toronto"? One way to keep costs down was to buy fabric directly from mills in England and Europe. And written proof shows that Walter Beauchamp Sr. did exactly that.

Walter wrote numerous letters to Viola during his buying trips to Europe in 1909 and 1910. Writing on January 11, 1909, aboard the ss *Haverford* of the Dominion Line, Walter reported that he would visit London, then Feltham (perhaps to visit family in Middlesex), Bradford (still a major textile-producing centre today), and eventually Paris, "if I don't change my mind." Despite the origin of his family name, Walter confessed to Viola that he was not all that fond of the French. Later that year, writing before another trip to Europe, this time on the White Star Line's ss *Laurentic*, he said that from then on "I will only go once a year," a comment that suggests he had already made many visits.

Although Walter and Alf were ambitious, business was slow but steady in the years before the First World War. On May 29, 1909, just six months after the company was incorporated, Walter wrote to Viola:

On board S.S. "Laurentic."

June 26/09

Dear Nia

Well we are near
the end of the Ocean
trip as we expect to
land in Liverpool tomorrow
morning, we have had
a very nice trip over
the weather has been
grand and a very nice
lot of passengers, we had
about fifty Mormons
on board but they dont
look a bit good to yours

"Business has only been fair this week, but we have to expect it now." Even so, just a week later, on June 5, he was pleased to announce that they had received "twenty orders so far this week, that is growing some, isn't it? But we need them in our business." Changing the store's location also seemed to be a stepping stone to success. Walter and Alf always knew that their first address was temporary. As it turned out, their friend Frank Burton would once again help them take their next step.

Whereas R. Score & Son dominated men's tailoring on King Street West, women's tailoring was centred at O'Brien's, whose space Walter and Alf shared at 73 King, along with Burton. Such close quarters led to a split in 1912, when Burton joined forces with O'Brien's head cutter, John Ahlgren, and some of his staff, and moved a few doors west to 97 King to start a company called Ahlgren's. Walter and Alf were not ready to take over the remaining space at 73 King, so they started looking for a new home. In the spring of 1914, a few months before the war broke out in Europe, Beauchamp & How moved to 97 King to share space with Ahlgren's. They would spend the next five years at that address, years that would not only cement Beauchamp & How in Canada's tailoring history but also shake the founda-tions of Canadian society. ⠒

A letter from Walter Beauchamp Sr. to Viola Mackenzie, June 26, 1909, written aboard the ss Laurentic *during one of Walter's buying trips to England. The White Star Line's* Laurentic *was a much smaller mechanical template for its ill-fated cousin the* Titanic. *The* Laurentic *also met an unfortunate end. Commissioned for use during the First World War, the ship struck two mines and sank in 1917.*

Walter Beauchamp Sr. (left), 1910.

MEN'S STYLES OF EDWARDIAN TORONTO

Early in the 1900s, Canada followed the styles and fashions of Britain, in particular, and of the United States. The dominant style in the Toronto market was the Victorian, and then the Edwardian, "sack" suit (sometimes referred to as "sacque"). It had supplanted the frock coat, which had been popular late in the nineteenth century in the eastern United States, as well as in Toronto. Instead of the four panels of fabric used to assemble the back of the frock coat, two panels are used for the jacket of a sack suit. In this way, the jacket is assembled more like a sack—not that it looks like one. In fact, it was originally based on a more casual coat style from France. This casual look initially limited the style to country pursuits, such as shooting and riding. But by the time Beauchamp & How launched its business in 1908, the sack suit was acceptable for business and city wear alike.

Edwardian styles did not stray far from their Victorian predecessors during the first decade of the twentieth century. By today's standards, sack jackets were quite long, falling well below the seat, which made the torso look long and slim. Edwardian jackets featured naturally shaped shoulders and a slightly nipped-in waist. The buttons on the front of the jacket were just a few inches apart (as opposed to about five inches today), allowing the lapels and the quarters (the bottoms of the jacket front) to swoop away elegantly. Though sack jackets were structured to ensure a shaped silhouette through the torso, they were far more relaxed than the tails and frock coats of the Victorian era.

Trousers, as well, were changing with the times, becoming slimmer at the ankle, almost to the point of caricature. "Peg-top" pants that tapered from about twenty-four inches at the knee to a mere sixteen inches at the cuff were much in vogue. (Today's suit pants are closer to twenty inches at the knee and eighteen inches at the cuff.) The peg-top style of pant had the unfortunate effect of making men look broad at the hips with tiny feet. Clearly one cannot account for fashion.

Much like the present day, 1908 saw seasonal changes and trends. Men were beginning to embrace colour in their wardrobes, moving away from the blacks and charcoals of the previous era. As the *Dry Goods Review* noted, pointing toward the spring trends of 1909, "olive drabs, olive browns and browns and blues" were finding favour. The Canadian magazine called these colours "extravagantly fancy" without being "extreme." In fact, the November issue declared: "Browns are

The Single-Breasted Sacque Suit

This is still the favored style for business and general wear.

We specialize our "Honley Blue Serge" at........$25.00

Other qualities up to............................ 35.00

Scotch tweeds, fancy cheviots and English worsteds are much worn. Prices range from......$25.00 **to** $40.00

R. SCORE & SON, LIMITED

The Double-Breasted Sacque Suit

This style still retains its popularity and looks equally well made from the celebrated "Honley Blue Serge," at. $25.00

Other qualities up to...................... 35.00

Or in Scotch tweeds, fancy cheviots and English worsteds. Prices range from.............$25.00 **to** $40.00

"THE HOUSE THAT QUALITY BUILT"

holding a strong place in suitings, but the opinion is it will never rank as a staple color," a statement that still holds true more than 100 years later.

In the nineteenth century, suiting could weigh more than twenty ounces a yard, which meant a three-piece suit could easily weigh more than five pounds (the lining alone was heavier than most suiting today). But, with no central heating during a cold Toronto winter, you would have been grateful for a warm, thick suit of serge or tweed. Even so, in the early part of the twentieth century, lighter fabrics—which had traditionally been used for women's clothing—were starting to migrate into men's tailoring. It was a trend Walter certainly took notice of, as did Viola. ⋮⋮

ABOVE *Among the styles popular at the time of Beauchamp & How's launch were single- and double-breasted sack (sacque) suits.*

A VISIT TO THE TORONTO ISLANDS, 1907

Was out on the bay in a gasoline boat yesterday and ... went over to the island at night, it is just as crazy as ever but the new park is not half bad and some of the amusements are very good there, such as the Chutes and Dip the Dip.
—Walter Beauchamp Sr., in a letter to Viola Mackenzie, July 23, 1907

Walter Sr.'s letters paint a detailed, personal view of the Toronto Islands early in the 1900s, but it's not a description that many Torontonians would recognize today. Long before the parkland, Centreville Amusement Park, and dragon boat races, the islands were a thriving suburb that welcomed throngs of visitors and hosted a large year-round population. Development on the islands included Victorian mansions, where the city's rich escaped the heat of summer, a tent community on Ward's Island, and a number of hotels. But by far the greatest attractions, the ones that drew Walter and his friends in 1907, were Hanlan's Point Amusement Park and Hanlan's Point Stadium.

The amusement park, opened in the mid-1890s, was Toronto's very own Coney Island and included numerous attractions, such as the ones mentioned in Walter's letter. Chute-the-Chutes (also Shoot-the-Chutes or Shooting-the-Shoots), the precursor to today's log flume and water slide, was extremely popular in amusement parks across Canada and the United States. The more complex version of the ride, in which a small boat shot down a greased track and into a small pool, operated at Scarboro Beach Amusement Park. The version at Hanlan's was a simple waterslide that emptied into the shallows of an Island beach. Dip the Dip, the forerunner of Coney Island's Wonder Wheel, promised "to combine all the thrills of the scenic railway, Ferris wheel and Chute-the-Chutes." Described as "a real thrill," the ride featured "dip" cars suspended on circular tracks within the Ferris wheel structure so that they would tip and fall at high speeds along the track as the wheel slowly revolved. The rides were meant for adults, and consequently an older crowd enjoyed the amusement parks, though some children were seen too.

In his letter of July 23, Walter, who evidently spent a fair amount of time on the islands, also writes: "I think we will go to the Lacrosse game on Saturday, haven't seen one this year yet and it is sure to be good. The Tecumsehs are ahead in the league and just Toronto and Buffalo are tied for first place in the baseball league so we have a good chance for both Championships this year."

Lacrosse was quite a popular sport in Toronto at the time. The games were played at Hanlan's Point Stadium, a massive round structure with partially covered stands that seated more than ten thousand spectators. Nestled against the amusement park on one side, with the lake on the other, the stadium had been built for lacrosse and baseball in 1903 after the previous stadium burned down. It was at these grounds (in another incarnation of the stadium) that the legendary baseball player Babe Ruth was to hit his first professional home run in 1914.

In 1907, as Walter was writing, one of the city's teams—the Toronto Tecumsehs, also known as the "Indians"—had suffered its first defeat of the lacrosse season at the hands of the Montreal Shamrocks the day before. Sadly for Walter, Montreal went on to win the league championship.

PREVIOUS *This postcard shows Hanlan's Point Amusement Park in the foreground and the large covered wraparound stands of the stadium behind.*

ABOVE *A photo of Hanlan's Point Amusement Park in 1911, taken by William James.*

FACING TOP *The Toronto Maple Leafs baseball team takes to the field at Hanlan's Point Stadium, ca. 1910.*

FACING BOTTOM *The Big Scream roller coaster was a prominent backdrop to Hanlan's Point Stadium, as seen in this photo from 1910.*

Meanwhile, the Toronto Maple Leafs baseball team, playing in the Eastern League (A level, just below major-league baseball), also went on to lose the championship. Some things about Toronto sports never change.

Walter Beauchamp Sr.'s love of sports was not confined to his youth; in addition to becoming one of Toronto's best-known tailors, he was also one of the city's best-known boxing and wrestling promoters in the 1920s and '30s. ∷

Boardroom to Battlefield:
Military Tailoring

Walter Beauchamp's is unique among Canadian tailors in that it has been both a civilian and military tailoring business for more than 100 years. The company began as a civilian tailor, with the occasional job producing uniforms for the Toronto Railway Company in the early years (see page 64),

but that balance changed drastically when war broke out in Europe in 1914. Most of Toronto's young men, numbering about seventy thousand, enlisted in the army. One in seven would not return from the First World War and countless others were seriously wounded. But the overwhelming

demand for dress uniforms led to an increase in the number of military tailors in Canada and the United Kingdom, prompting Walter and Alf to step up production at Beauchamp & How as part of their civic duty. Eventually they would produce almost all of the Royal Flying Corps uniforms ordered for RFC men stationed in Canada. These included full-dress uniforms and officer's tunics.

During the First World War, the company established traditions that were passed down from Walter Sr. to his son Walter Jr. and eventually to grandson Terry: soldiers always received the best possible price; Beauchamp's gladly held on to an unfinished garment when a soldier was deployed; and a down payment was never requested. Walter Sr.'s watchword came down through three generations of Beauchamp tailors: "It is our duty to look after those who serve our country."

In the early days of the business, even though Walter Beauchamp Sr. was regarded as an astute and successful businessman, he was not a member of Toronto's elite. Not, that is, until 1912, when he married Viola Mackenzie, whose many connections in high places helped establish Beauchamp & How. It was not a marriage of convenience, however, as Walter and Viola had

FACING *A 1970 watercolour print of* The Rifleman, *ca. 1885. A metal plaque on the frame reads: "Presented to Walter Beauchamp regimental tailor to Queen's Own Rifles of Canada by the Officers, 1976."*

ABOVE *Viola and Walter Beauchamp Sr. on their wedding day, October 10, 1912, with two unidentified bridesmaids and a groomsman.*

begun courting long before tailoring entered the picture. But that family connection was the link to the military regiment with which Beauchamp's has been most indelibly associated for almost as long as the company has been in business: the Queen's Own Rifles of Canada.

Viola's uncle, Sir William Mackenzie, was the man behind the Toronto Railway Company (see page 64), and one of that

company's directors was Sir Henry Pellatt, the man who would go on to build Toronto's iconic Casa Loma as his residence in 1914. Pellatt also formed the Electrical Development Company in 1903 to bring electricity to the rapidly expanding metropolis in partnership with Mackenzie (Beauchamp & How would later tailor uniforms for the Toronto Hydro-Electric System, thanks to this relationship). Through the Mackenzie family,

Beauchamp & How came to the attention of Pellatt. This link was serendipitous because Pellatt was also the commander of the Queen's Own Rifles of Canada from 1901 to 1920, eventually achieving the rank of Major General upon retirement.

Pellatt was an extremely wealthy man at the turn of the century and was knighted in 1905. To mark his regiment's fiftieth anniversary in 1910, he financed an extraordinary voyage. As he put it: "I wish to mark the Jubilee Year of The Queen's Own by some memorable event. The Queen's Own has given splendid service to Canada and to Toronto and deserves every recognition." He sailed to England with the entire regiment, more than six hundred soldiers and personnel, including all the officers' horses, for a six-week sojourn at Aldershot Garrison. At this popular training ground in Hampshire in the southeast of England, the regiment engaged in a series of military exercises, mock battles, and formal ceremonies and dined lavishly, all at Pellatt's expense. Even though no records show that Beauchamp & How made any military or civilian garments for Pellatt, his son, Reginald, who also became commanding officer of the Queen's Own Rifles of Canada, did have a full-dress uniform made by the firm in June of 1927.

FACING *A dress tunic tailored by Beauchamp & How in June 1921. This tunic was made for Lieutenant Colonel Reginald Pellatt, son of Sir Henry Pellatt (pictured right), when he was appointed Commanding Officer of the 2nd Battalion, Queen's Own Rifles of Canada.*

ABOVE *Sir Henry Pellatt wearing the full-dress uniform of the Queen's Own Rifles of Canada, 1910.*

Beauchamp's tailoring process has been fundamentally the same for civilian and military customers alike throughout its history. The individual is measured, the cloth is cut, and the garment is assembled. Even so, whereas in civilian tailoring the style and details are guided by individual taste and preference, these play no role whatsoever in military tailoring. And it may come as a surprise to anyone not familiar with the Armed Forces that, apart from combat gear, officers (as opposed to enlisted men and women) are responsible for procuring their own uniforms. They must pay for any regimental dress and any formal clothing out of their own pocket. They need two types of formal clothing, which are mandatory for officers: the full-dress uniform and mess dress.

Full dress is worn during ceremonies and official receptions and can be custom made or handed down from previously serving soldiers. Originally a day-to-day uniform, full dress was replaced by the more practical battle uniform and became purely ceremonial by the twentieth century. Mess dress, on the other hand, is an officer's evening wear, to be used at formal functions.

Both full dress and mess kits are predominantly custom made, with each

regiment dictating the colour of the fabric, the cut of the garment, and the exact nature and placement of the regalia. Not only do these tailoring guidelines vary widely from regiment to regiment, but they are also updated on occasion. But an update does not mean all officers must order an entirely new wardrobe. Only newly commissioned officers must have garments made to the latest specifications.

FACING *An illustration of mess dress from* The Cutter's Practical Guide to British Military Service Uniforms.

ABOVE LEFT *A No. 1 Service Dress ordered by Lieutenant Colonel I.M. Macdonell on March 15, 1934. In May of 1939, Lieutenant Colonel Macdonell was presented to His Majesty King George VI as Commanding Officer of the Queen's Own Rifles of Canada, during the royal visit to Toronto.*

ABOVE RIGHT *Lieutenant Colonel I.M. Macdonell, MBE, VD, ca. First World War.*

Air Publication 1358

DRESS REGULATIONS

for

OFFICERS OF THE
ROYAL AIR FORCE

FIRST EDITION
MAY
1929

LONDON:
PRINTED AND PUBLISHED BY HIS MAJESTY'S STATIONERY OFFICE
To be purchased directly from H.M. STATIONERY OFFICE at the following addresses:
Adastral House, Kingsway, London, W.C.2; 120, George Street, Edinburgh;
York Street, Manchester; 1, St. Andrew's Crescent, Cardiff;
15, Donegall Square West, Belfast;
or through any Bookseller.

1929
Price 4s. 6d. *net.*

22-101

Beauchamp & Haw Limited

For

5. *Officers of Auxiliary Air Force.*
(i) Description—A letter " A " in gilt metal. For greatcoat, $\frac{1}{2}$ in. in height ; and for tunic or jacket, $\frac{3}{8}$ in. in height.
(ii) Dresses on which worn and position.
(*a*) Full Dress—On shoulder straps of tunic, $\frac{1}{2}$ in. above the eagle and in a central position.
(*b*) Greatcoat when worn with Full and Mess Dress—On shoulder straps $\frac{1}{8}$ in. above the eagle and in a central position.
(*c*) Service Dress—On collar of jacket one inch above inner end of opening of step, midway between the outer edge and the inner (rolled) edge, placed in such a way that a line drawn through the centre of the badge is parallel to the inner (rolled) edge.
(*d*) Greatcoat when worn with Service Dress—On shoulder straps. For ranks Squadron Leader and above $\frac{1}{4}$ in. above top row of lace, and for ranks Flight Lieutenant and below $1\frac{1}{2}$ in. from bottom of shoulder strap to bottom of letter.

(*e*) Mess Dress—On shoulder straps $\frac{1}{8}$ in. above the eagle in a central position.
(iii) Medical Officers—Badge is worn $\frac{1}{8}$ in. below the medical badge on the Service and Mess Dress jackets. In Full Dress and on the greatcoat it is worn as at (ii) (*a*), (*b*), and (*d*) above.
(iv) Chaplains of the Auxiliary Air Force— Position $\frac{1}{8}$ in. above chaplain's collar badge on Service Dress.

6. *Armlets.*
(i) Provost Marshal, Royal Air Force. Cloth, $3\frac{1}{2}$ in. wide, consisting of alternate bands of black, red and black. Black letters " P. M." $\frac{3}{4}$ in. in height on centre band, surmounted by eagle in gilt metal and gold embroidered crown. Worn on right arm.
(ii) Assistant Provost Marshals, Royal Air Force. As for (i), except that letters " A.P.M." are substituted for " P.M."

Medical Off Collar Badges – bottom 1" above the inner end of the step opening the staff of Badge to be parallel to the inside Rolled edge

Chaplains Collar Badges – centre of the bottom of the badge 1" above the inner end of the step opening of the collar. upright of the cross parallel to the inside edge.

Badge A. & V.R. on Ser Jacket.
Medical Off. '/8 below Med Badge Dental '/8 below Badge.
Chaplain '/8 above Badge.
Other Officers – on Collar of Jacket 1" above inner end of step opening.
Badge A & VR on Greatcoats
on sh straps as follows.
S/Ld and above. midway between the top & bottom edges of Rank Braid
S/Ld and below. bottom of the letter contiguous (touching) with the bottom edge of the rank Braid
VR in 3/8 & '/2"

(See N & A uniform Book page 57)

FACING *The cover page from* Dress Regulations for Officers of the Royal Air Force.

ABOVE *Notes and additions written by Alf How in* Dress Regulations for Officers of the Royal Air Force.

RIGHT *The full-dress uniform of
the Toronto Scottish Regiment, 1951.*

FACING *The full-dress uniform of the
48th Highlanders, 1951.*

Finding a tailor who is familiar with uniform guidelines is key. And since the days of the First World War, Beauchamp's has been in possession of the most up-to-date tailoring specifications for all of Canada's regiments. Along with its know-how and experience, the company's understanding of regalia and its placement is one of the main reasons that Walter Beauchamp has become the tailor of choice for members of the Canadian Armed Forces.

"Choice" is the key word because, despite the fact that full dress and mess kits are mandatory, the military has no official tailor. Instead, soldiers must seek their own. Over many generations, word of mouth has sent legions of soldiers through the doors of Beauchamp's, including members of the Queen's Own Rifles of Canada, the Royal Regiment of Canada, the Governor General's Horse Guards, the 48th Highlanders of Canada, the Toronto Scottish Regiment, Princess Patricia's Canadian Light Infantry, the Hastings and Prince Edward Regiment, the Lincoln and Welland Regiment, and the Royal Hamilton Light Infantry, as well as members of the Navy and the Air Force.

In 1946, after the Second World War, Beauchamp & How referred to its dual identity as a "Civil and Military Tailor" for the first time. In the advertisements of subsequent years, Beauchamp's targeted the young man returning from war "as he steps back into business or professional life." In fact, the company emphasized its military tailoring as an advantage, to set Beauchamp & How apart from other civilian tailors. To this day, few other tailors in Canada, if any, have the knowledge and experience to create the exquisite detailing that military garments demand. For generations, the need to ensure that every stitch, every button, and every collar of a military garment are perfect has forced Beauchamp's tailors to maintain a high standard in all their work. That attention to detail is the key ingredient that makes its way into the company's civilian tailoring too.

"Our military tailoring tradition," says Terry Beauchamp, "is probably what I'm most proud of in my career and the life of this company." ::

FACING The mess kit ordered from Beauchamp & How by Major Harry T. Tye of the Governor General's Horse Guards on October 25, 1954.

ABOVE Eleanor "Billie" Mann, Honorary Colonel of the Ontario Regiment—among the oldest continuously serving reserve regiments in Canada—in her mess kit tailored by Walter Beauchamp.

OVERLEAF A Canadian Machine Gun Corps mess kit ordered from Beauchamp & How on October 3, 1930, by Major George Elliott Lucas.

THE RFC TUNIC OF J.W. BISHOP, DECEMBER 10, 1917

At the end of 1916, the First World War was mired in bloody trench warfare, making airborne power ever more valuable to the British forces. Brits, Canadians, and Americans were all clamouring to join the battle in the air. But England did not have the room or the resources for additional training facilities and airplane factories, so it turned to the colonies. The Royal Flying Corps Canada (RFCC) was formed in the spring of 1917 and tasked with training more pilots. James Armishaw heard the call and enlisted.

Armishaw was a British subject who had emigrated to the United States in 1907. A decade later, he was living with his wife and daughter in Alden, New York (just east of Buffalo), and working as a truck driver, but he decided to cross the border into Canada and enlist. He was immediately put to work as a driver for the Flying Corps' paymaster, Major Bowler, in downtown Toronto. Having the lowest rank of "aircraftman," Armishaw was not eligible for, nor could he afford, a tailored uniform. But, with so many pilots coming through the RFCC training schools (more than three thousand by the end of the war), used tunics were not hard to come by. Armishaw was given a tunic that had originally been made for an American, John Wallis Bishop, in 1917 by Beauchamp & How. Bishop, after completing his training in

Canada, had been shipped overseas for fourteen months and went on to fly numerous missions over the Italian front.

The tunic left behind by Bishop and eventually worn by Armishaw, but without pilot's badges or markings, was the standard-issue dress of the Royal Flying Corps. Also known simply as a "service jacket," the tunic was special in a number of ways.

Its design, a long, flared coat with a deep centre vent, worn with breeches, was based on the British cavalry uniforms of the late nineteenth century, because the RFC airmen were called the "mounted squadrons of the air." The tunic was also known colloquially as the "maternity jacket" because the jacket's flared skirt evoked the clothes worn by the expectant mothers of that era. ⁝⁝

FACING *Aircraftman James Armishaw wearing a service jacket tailored by Beauchamp & How in 1917, photographed in 1918.*

ABOVE *A Royal Flying Corps service jacket tailored by Beauchamp & How in 1917, worn by Aircraftman James Armishaw.*

OVERLEAF *Detailed instructions for cutting and constructing a Royal Flying Corps service jacket from* The Cutter's Practical Guide to British Military Service Uniforms.

out of the base of neck in consequence of the wide overlap at the breast. The front overlap is an important feature.

In the sealed pattern (medium size) the buttons were placed 12 inches from the edge at top and 7 inches at the waist. There are five buttons a side, and the left or overlapping edge is finished by a fly. Fly-stitching does not show through, and there is an average of $3\frac{1}{2}$-inch spacing between holes and buttons. To attain this end, cut $6\frac{1}{2}$ inches of peak on at top front, 4 inches at waist, increasing it to 5 inches at the bottom. Edges and seams are swelled $\frac{1}{4}$in. wide, and the cuff is quite plain, and devoid of stitching. It will be necessary to cut the collars on the bias, and to well draw the crease. The inner stand is stitched with five rows of machine stitching. The right front edge of coat is devoid of hooks, jigger button or holes. It should be noted that the top button is $3\frac{1}{2}$ inches down, and that the peak is held securely by a substantial hook. Buttons are ring-edge ivory four holes to match. There is an inside left breast pocket.

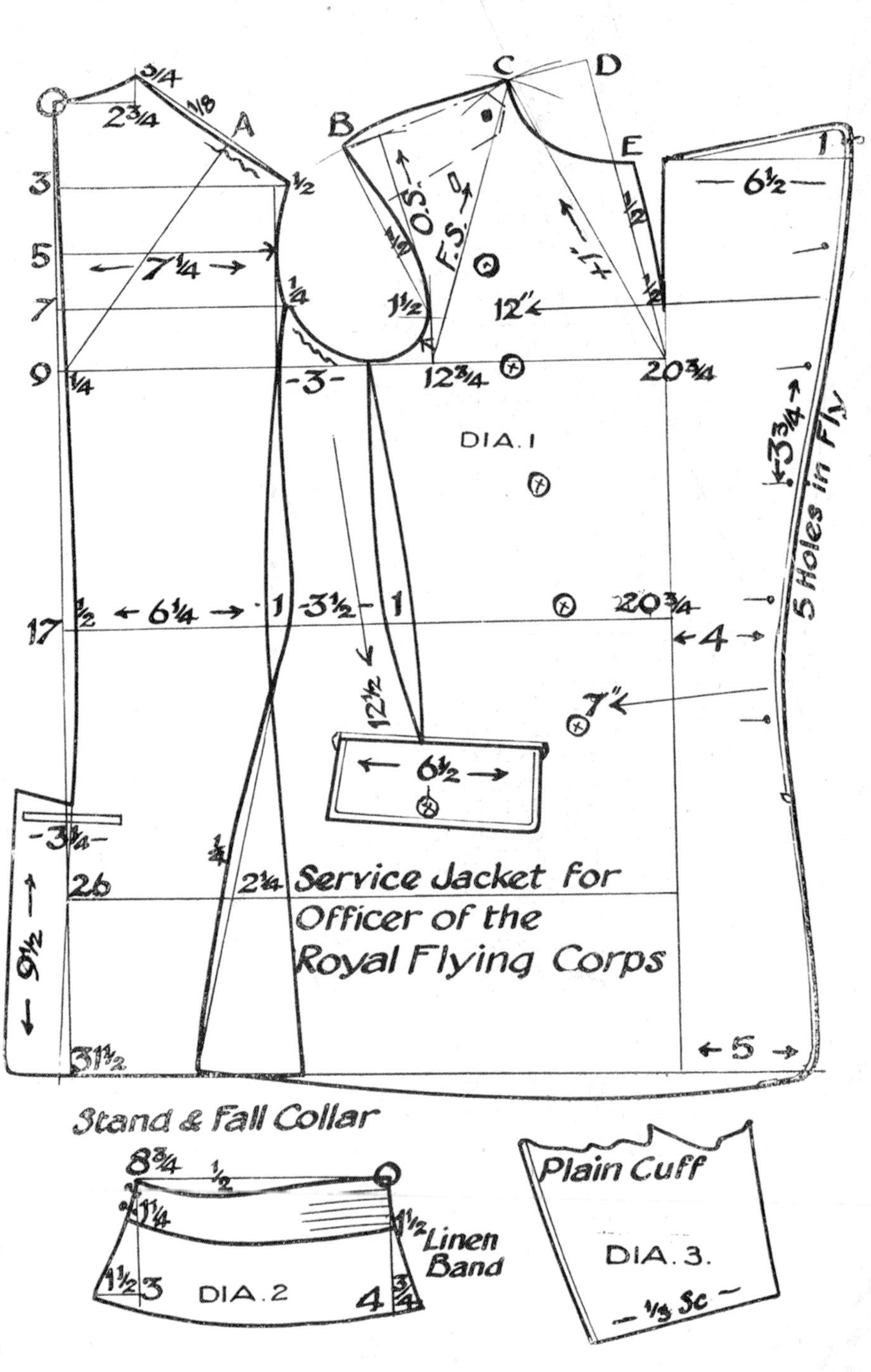

THE SYSTEM.

Rule line O $31\frac{1}{2}$, the average length for a 5ft. 8in. figure.

O to 3 one-third of scye depth, to 9 the scye depth, to waist 17 inches, to 26 9 inches lower for seat prominence.

Square out from each point.

Divide 3 to 9 into three parts.

Go in $\frac{1}{2}$in. at waist and draw back-seam, and add the slit 2 inches wide, as shown.

O to $2\frac{3}{4}$ one-third of neck. (The circumference of neck is made 1 inch more than the size of linen collar usually worn, thus for a 36-inch chest man wearing a $15\frac{1}{2}$ collar, the neck size is $16\frac{1}{2}$, half of which is used for working the system, and hereafter termed the neck, $8\frac{1}{4}$ inches.)

Apply the back width, plus two seams, on line 5, and square line up from breast line to meet this measure.

Add $\frac{1}{4}$in. on line 7 and $\frac{1}{2}$in. on line 3 for back shape.

From $\frac{1}{4}$ to $20\frac{3}{4}$ measure the half chest plus $2\frac{1}{2}$ inches.

Go back 8 inches, the across chest, and raise $1\frac{1}{2}$in. as shown.

Sweep C from $12\frac{3}{4}$ by the front shoulder less the back neck.

Add 1 inch to this measure and sweep again from $20\frac{3}{4}$, and so find the neckpoint.

Sweep B from $12\frac{3}{4}$ by the over-shoulder measure less the distance from A to $\frac{1}{4}$.

Make C to B $\frac{1}{4}$in. less than the length of back shoulder.

Shape the scye.

C to D one-third of neck, $2\frac{3}{4}$ inches.

Square C D by $20\frac{3}{4}$, and go down from D to E one-third of neck plus $\frac{1}{2}$in.

Place the vee, E, $\frac{1}{2}$in. outside the centre line.

Square down from $20\frac{3}{4}$.

Continue this line up outside E, and take out a $\frac{3}{4}$in. vee.

Square out $6\frac{1}{2}$ inches, and draw the front edge exactly as shown; also mark the holes and buttons.

Make the width of back at waist one-sixth of breast plus $\frac{1}{4}$in., or 1 inch less than the distance from back-seam to scye on line 5, and from 26 let the width be increased 1 inch, or $7\frac{1}{4}$ inches. Finish back.

Take out 1 inch at waist and overlap the front 2 inches on seat line.

Add $\frac{1}{4}$in. of round.

Mark the fish one-sixth of scale, and one-sixth plus $\frac{1}{2}$in. at waist, taking out 1 inch or so, according to the size of waist.

In large-waisted figures $20\frac{3}{4}$ will be ad-

Beauchamp & Haw Limited

SERVICE JACKET, ROYAL ARMY FLYING CORPS.

vanced one-sixth of disproportion before measuring up the waist.

The pockets are placed 1½in. back from the line of buttons, and made 6½ to 7 inches long and 2½ inches deep.

Diagram 2 shows the cutting of the collar. O, 8¾, the neck, plus ½in.

Hollow sewing edge ½in., as shown.

Square to 4, which quantity includes 1½in. for stand and 2½ inches for fall.

Add ¾in. of spring to the back-seam.

Square down at 8¾ inches ½in. less than back depth, and go out 1½in. for point as shown.

The stand is cut 1¼in. high at the front.

As will be seen, this collar is practically straight and needs ample manipulation and pressing to ensure a snug fit.

"BRITISH WARMERS."

The Pea Jacket, blue and khaki, are commonly termed "British Warms" by military men. These garments are recognized units of the officer's kit, and have recently become very popular.

The pattern garments at the War Office date from 1908, and are still in vogue.

Official instructions are given on the sealed tickets attached as follows:

Pea Jacket.—May be worn by general and staff officers at home, who wear the blue service dress in bivouacs, on night work generally, and at other times when a warm coat is required, and the wearing of the regular greatcoat is not desirable.

Khaki.—May be worn by general and staff officers abroad, and by all other officers at home and abroad, and in similar conditions to the Pea Jacket, blue, when the drab service dress is worn by general and staff officers, under provision of the "Note" in paragraph 39 of the dress regulations, which stipulate that all officers in a unit must be dressed alike.

From the above it will be seen that these are overgarments, and must, therefore, be cut as such, providing ample ease for fitting comfortably over the service dress, and as the fittings of the latter vary somewhat, such as the number of pockets, pleats, etc., it is well to consider this when taking orders for these coats, for they must have plenty of room.

The blue cloth is of a heavy soft finish, which should not prove difficult to match, but we were informed that such was not the case with the Khaki, as it is much lighter in shade than that usually met with. Strictly speaking it is not khaki, but more of a light silver-sand shade.

In shape they resemble the Naval Reefer, buttoning high, with three buttons, and hav-

THE MESS KIT OF LIEUTENANT C.O. DALTON, 1931

Charles Osborne Dalton enlisted as a cadet at age fifteen with the Queen's Own Rifles of Canada Cadet Corps. Only six years later, in 1931, at the ripe old age of twenty-one, Dalton became an officer and purchased his very first custom-made mess kit at Beauchamp & How.

During the Second World War, Dalton had reached the rank of major and was tasked with helping to lead the operations on D-Day, June 6, 1944, the largest seaborne invasion in military history. As commander of B company, Major Dalton landed on the beaches of Bernières-sur-Mer, France, with 120 of his men. As he told it, the experience was harrowing:

> When I said, "Follow me!" and dashed down the ramp into 12 feet of water, I disappeared. I had an 85-pound pack on my back with ammunition and food and so on, plus I had a life preserver on, so we all sank just like stones. So when people say we ran up the beach, I say: "Run? I was barely crawling up the beach!" The man next to me was hit seven times down his arm. I didn't get touched.
>
> We scrambled up the beach, and when I looked back I was horrified to see that there was nobody following me.

FACING *The mess kit ordered by Lieutenant C.O. Dalton on October 18, 1931, from Beauchamp & How.*

ABOVE *Colonel Charles Osborne Dalton, DSO, KStJ, ED.*

I thought they had gone to ground, but in fact they were lying at the water's edge and Germans were firing at them as they lay wounded. So in 10 minutes, of the 120 men I had with me, we were all either killed or wounded…

The pillbox I was assigned to attack was supposed to have been taken out by the Engineers and the Tank Corps, but that didn't happen because it was too rough and the tanks tended to sink right off the landing craft. I had a ladder that we put up the wall, and then I fired at the shield with the hope that the bullets would ricochet off them and fly around inside their pillbox. And actually they did, so the machine guns stopped firing, but we were still no closer to getting in.

Meanwhile, one of the German officers got his 9 mm revolver out and fired at me and it drilled through my helmet and down the ladder I slid. It was about 8:30 in the morning, I guess, and I was walking along the beach trying to catch up with the rest of the company. A medical officer saw the bandage on my head and he took the dressing off and put another bigger one on. He said, "You will be back in England by tonight," but I wasn't back in England that night, I was lying on stretcher on the beach until 3 o'clock in the morning.

So on the third day we were put on a tank transporter, which was a large landing craft, and we were stacked up three high on stretchers. By that time, cigarettes were getting pretty scarce, but here's the kind of comradeship we had. I would light a cigarette and take two puffs and then pass it to the man above me who took two puffs. And if nobody cheated, it would go all the way up to the top rack and back

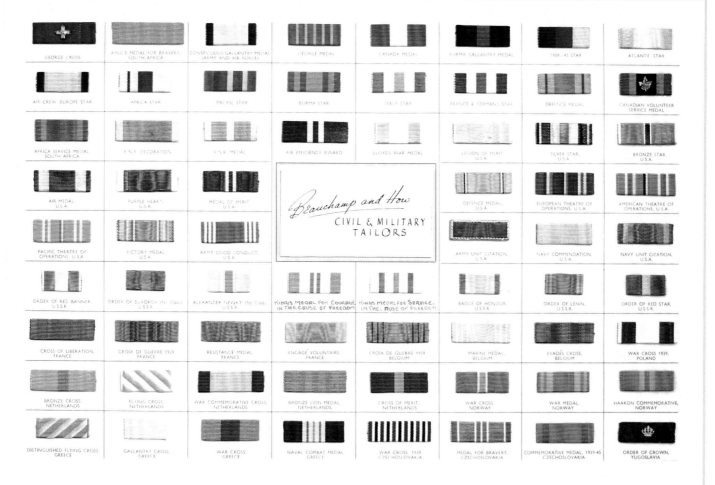

The grid of medal ribbons, left to right, top to bottom, reads:

GEORGE CROSS | KING'S MEDAL FOR BRAVERY, SOUTH AFRICA | CONSPICUOUS GALLANTRY MEDAL (ARMY AND AIR FORCE) | GEORGE MEDAL | CANADA MEDAL | BURMA GALLANTRY MEDAL | 1939—45 STAR | ATLANTIC STAR

AIR CREW EUROPE STAR | AFRICA STAR | PACIFIC STAR | BURMA STAR | ITALY STAR | FRANCE & GERMANY STAR | DEFENCE MEDAL | CANADIAN VOLUNTEER SERVICE MEDAL

AFRICA SERVICE MEDAL, SOUTH AFRICA | R.N.R. DECORATION | R.N.R. MEDAL | AIR EFFICIENCY AWARD | LLOYD'S WAR MEDAL | LEGION OF MERIT, U.S.A. | SILVER STAR, U.S.A. | BRONZE STAR, U.S.A.

AIR MEDAL, U.S.A. | PURPLE HEART, U.S.A. | MEDAL OF MERIT, U.S.A. | *Beauchamp and How* CIVIL & MILITARY TAILORS | DEFENCE MEDAL, U.S.A. | EUROPEAN THEATRE OF OPERATIONS, U.S.A. | AMERICAN THEATRE OF OPERATIONS, U.S.A.

PACIFIC THEATRE OF OPERATIONS, U.S.A. | VICTORY MEDAL, U.S.A. | ARMY GOOD CONDUCT, U.S.A. | | ARMY UNIT CITATION, U.S.A. | NAVY COMMENDATION, U.S.A. | NAVY UNIT CITATION, U.S.A.

ORDER OF RED BANNER, U.S.S.R. | ORDER OF SUVOROV (1st Class), U.S.S.R. | ALEXANDER NEVSKY (1st Class), U.S.S.R. | KING'S MEDAL FOR COURAGE, IN THE CAUSE OF FREEDOM | KING'S MEDAL FOR SERVICE, IN THE CAUSE OF FREEDOM | BADGE OF HONOUR, U.S.S.R. | ORDER OF LENIN, U.S.S.R. | ORDER OF RED STAR, U.S.S.R.

CROSS OF LIBERATION, FRANCE | CROIX DE GUERRE 1939, FRANCE | RESISTANCE MEDAL, FRANCE | ENGAGÉ VOLUNTAIRE, FRANCE | CROIX DE GUERRE 1939, BELGIUM | MARINE MEDAL, BELGIUM | EVADÉS CROSS, BELGIUM | WAR CROSS 1939, POLAND

BRONZE CROSS, NETHERLANDS | FLYING CROSS, NETHERLANDS | WAR COMMEMORATIVE CROSS, NETHERLANDS | BRONZE LION MEDAL, NETHERLANDS | CROSS OF MERIT, NETHERLANDS | WAR CROSS, NORWAY | WAR MEDAL, NORWAY | HAAKON COMMEMORATIVE, NORWAY

DISTINGUISHED FLYING CROSS, GREECE | GALLANTRY CROSS, GREECE | WAR CROSS, GREECE | NAVAL COMBAT MEDAL, GREECE | WAR CROSS, 1939, CZECHOSLOVAKIA | MEDAL FOR BRAVERY, CZECHOSLOVAKIA | COMMEMORATIVE MEDAL, 1939-45, CZECHOSLOVAKIA | ORDER OF CROWN, YUGOSLAVIA

down and I would get the last puff. Well, most people would say, "Here I am, and I don't even know if I'm going to be alive by morning, so I'm going to take a really good drag on it," but nobody did.

Dalton remained with the Queen's Own Rifles of Canada for the rest of his military career, retiring in 1975 with the rank of Colonel. He died in Toronto on February 21, 1999, at the age of eighty-eight. ⁝⁝

FACING A portrait of Lieutenant Charles Osborne Dalton painted by Archibald Bruce Stapleton.

ABOVE A collection of Canadian war-medal ribbons produced as a tailor's guide and a showpiece for the Beauchamp & How store in 1951.

OVERLEAF The dress tunic worn by Major General Malcolm Smith Mercer as Commanding Officer of the Queen's Own Rifles of Canada during the First World War. Major General Mercer was killed in Flanders on June 2, 1916. To this day he remains the highest-ranking Canadian officer killed in action.

THE FROCK COAT OF LIEUTENANT D.A. FITZGERALD, 1938

When Captain P.J. VanAuken was named the Director of Music for the Governor General's Horse Guards in 2010, she was given many responsibilities. For instance, she had to conduct the full brass and reed military band even though she had never conducted before. But she was also given something that would help her in her duties: a frock coat that had belonged to a previous music director and had been kept throughout the years.

The coat had been made decades earlier for Lieutenant D.A. Fitzgerald, still known affectionately as "Fitz." Because it hadn't been worn by anyone except its original owner, it was in excellent condition. And even though the small coat had been custom made for a man, it fit Captain VanAuken surprisingly well. Wearing it, she could feel the spirit of those who had come before her, a spirit that inspires her to this day.

The frock coat did need a few alterations, though. As a long-time customer of Beauchamp's, Captain VanAuken did not hesitate to entrust the garment to Terry. He was immediately impressed by its quality and construction, especially its quilted lining, something he had rarely seen. But they were both pleasantly surprised when Terry looked inside the breast pocket and discovered from the tailor's tag that the coat had been made in December of 1938 by none other than Beauchamp & How. ⁚⁚

ABOVE Captain P.J. VanAuken wearing the frock coat given to music directors of the Governor General's Horse Guards. The coat was originally tailored by Beauchamp & How for Lieutenant D.A. Fitzgerald in December 1938 and was altered by Walter Beauchamp Tailors to fit Captain VanAuken when she was appointed as Director of Music for the GGHG in 2010.

THE GREATCOAT OF COLONEL
A.J. EVERETT, 1940

In the fall of 2006, a man walked into Walter Beauchamp Tailors with a Second World War greatcoat in remarkably fine condition. But he hadn't brought it in for alteration or repair. He had found the greatcoat at an estate auction, noticed the tag that named the maker as Beauchamp & How, and wondered whether it could be connected to Walter Beauchamp Tailors. Terry immediately recognized the coat's quality and historical importance and bought it on the spot, returning the greatcoat to the place where it had started its life. What Terry didn't know was the coat's pedigree and its connection to Canadian military history.

Inside the breast pocket of the coat was the tailor's tag with the date the customer had been measured: December 23, 1940. The customer's name on the tag was "Col. A.J. Everett." Terry's curiosity was piqued, so he enlisted the help of his friend and customer Chief Warrant Officer Scott Patterson of the Queen's Own Rifles of Canada. Patterson was also a military historian and had some insights as soon as he saw the garment. The cut suggested a mounted regiment and the pattern dated from before the Second World War, indicating that Colonel Everett had served before 1940, possibly even in the First World War. He was right on both counts.

Arthur James Everett had joined the Armed Forces at the age of seventeen in 1908 and served in the Canadian Expeditionary Force during the First World War. In the interwar years, Everett had risen to the position of Commanding Officer of the Governor General's Body Guard, a mounted regiment. When that regiment merged with the Mississauga Horse to form the Governor General's Horse Guards in 1936, Everett became Commanding Officer of the new regiment. He retired from active service soon after, in 1937, but his role in the Armed Forces was far from over.

In a supremely prescient act in the fall of 1938—one year before the outbreak of war in Europe—Everett began calling for "universal military service" in Canada. The Dominion, he argued, could not "maintain her national independence and her identity as a self-governing nation" by relying on the United States or the United Kingdom to fight on her behalf. And Everett saw other advantages to a standing civilian army: "Those serving would gain physically from the training, they would learn discipline and self-respect, and... they would develop a love of country which seems so lacking in boys who have had a stupid brand of pacifism drilled into them." He finished a series of speeches and articles with a prophetic warning: "For us to remain neutral in the event of war just isn't possible, and if we can't be neutral we must be ready."

When war broke out, Everett was indeed ready. By the end of 1940 he had been promoted to Colonel and appointed Director of Mobilization and Recruiting. It was then that he visited Beauchamp's (a few months after the death of Alf How) and ordered his greatcoat. By late 1942, Colonel Everett was no longer in Toronto but stationed in Halifax as the Assistant Adjutant and Quartermaster General at Atlantic Command headquarters.

Colonel Arthur James Everett died in Toronto on April 5, 1983. ⁝⁝

ABOVE *An undated photo of Colonel A.J. Everett, ca. 1940s.*

OVERLEAF *A Second World War greatcoat ordered by Lieutenant Colonel A.J. Everett from Beauchamp & How on December 23, 1940.*

TO THE CUTTING OF MILITARY GARMENTS.

THE MILITARY TUNICS OF ASSISTANT SECTION OFFICER M. CHASE, 1943

In the spring of 2010, a receipt was returned to Walter Beauchamp Tailors after nearly seven decades. Robert Gibson had found a Beauchamp & How receipt for two military tunics worn by his recently deceased mother, Margaret Olena Gibson (née Chase). Gibson felt that returning the receipts to the tailor would bring his mother's story full circle. He also presented Terry Beauchamp with a short memoir he had helped his mother write. It painted a detailed personal view of the lives of women who served in the Canadian military during the war.

In 1940, the Canadian government announced it was forming women's units in the armed services. Margaret Chase found herself torn. Her Quaker background dictated that as a true pacifist she should ignore the call. That being said, fighting for Canada was also in her blood. Her uncle, Lieutenant Colonel Walter Brown, had led the 4th Brigade of the Canadian Field Artillery regiment (now the Royal Regiment of Canadian Artillery) in the First World War. And her great-grandfather had fought at Lundy's Lane, one of the bloodiest battles of the War of 1812. So, on the first Saturday that the enlistment offices were open, Chase signed on at the Royal Canadian Air Force office in Toronto. Having worked as a physical education teacher, Chase was told she'd most likely

FACING *The dress and activities of Boy Scouts in 1913, according to* The Cutter's Practical Guide to British Military Service Uniforms.

ABOVE *A portrait photograph of Margaret Chase wearing one of the two dress tunics tailored for her by Beauchamp & How in 1943.*

be doing the same for the army. Though that was not how she wanted to serve her country, it was too late to back out—she'd already handed in her forms.

When Margaret Chase was finally called up in March of 1942, she and the other women recruits reported to No. 6 Manning Depot (previously the site of Havergal College) on Jarvis Street in Toronto as airwomen second class (AW2C). After six weeks of basic training, she was off to St. Thomas, Ontario, to learn everything she could about air force equipment, from clothing and kitchen utensils to airplanes and trucks. Chase, like many other female university graduates from across Canada, was trained to manage supply stores for the air force across the country.

Chase spent the next six months in Aylmer, Ontario, as the equipment manager of an air force training school. The work was complex and tedious, and she was far

from the front. But she excelled at it and was soon transferred again, back to the large training school in Toronto. She was promoted to sergeant and given the task of looking after thousands of dollars' worth of station equipment.

In mid-1943, Chase was removed from inventory duty. She became assistant section 48 officer (ASO) and was posted to No. 3 Flying Instructors School in Arnprior, Ontario, where she spent the next couple of years helping retrain returning fighter pilots to become instructors. Her work also included jobs not in the description, such as arranging weddings and funerals and, when pilots went missing, telephoning people who lived north of the Ottawa River to ask whether they had seen a plane fly over.

It was at her post in Arnprior that Chase's story intersected with Beauchamp & How. As an ASO, Chase could have two uniforms tailor made. She asked her uncle, now Colonel Brown, for advice. Since the First World War, he had always shopped at Beauchamp & How, and he vouched for the company's quality and knowledge. Margaret Chase headed to the shop and had two tunics made—a dark one and a light one—for twenty-five dollars each.

OUR ORDER NO. <u>1845</u>

TELEPHONE ELGIN 3875

Beauchamp and How Limited

91 King Street West   TORONTO,

September 16th, 1943.

A/S/O M.O. Chase,
#2, K.T.S. Jarvis St.,
Toronto 2, Ontario.

CONVEYANCE

PRICES NET CASH, NO DISCOUNT ALLOWED

To Tunic and Skirt	50	00	50	00
Sept. 16th Cash			25	—
			25	—

BEAUCHAMP & HOW LIMITED
91 KING STREET WEST
TORONTO 1, ONT.

TORONTO
SEP 23
8 30 PM
1943
ONTARIO

UNITED WELFARE
FUND
CAMPAIGNS III ONE

CANADA
POSTES POSTAGE
3 CENTS

3 F.I.S.

R.C.A.F.   *Amplw. Ont.*

TORONTO
SEP 24
8 30 PM
1943
ONTARIO

CONSERVE COAL
SAVE
ONE TON

After D-Day, Chase took on her most emotionally challenging job. She was sent to air force headquarters in Ottawa to work on bringing 48,000 war brides to Canada, along with their 22,000 children. Chase spent the next two years immersed in endless immigration paperwork and dealing with families desperate to be reunited. She made countless trips from Ottawa to Pier 21 in Halifax, where the brides landed after their ocean crossing. Most were unaware that they would then face days of train travel, with small children in tow, across a country much bigger than their homeland.

Early one morning in midwinter, while taking the train through Quebec, Chase was woken up by an irate and concerned train agent. "Ma'am, get up and get those girls in," he said, pointing out the window at three young brides dancing in the snow in their pajamas and rejoicing in the fresh air. "They haven't any clothes on and it's twenty-eight below zero."

But the episode that stood out most for Chase was a train trip early in 1945. Once again she was escorting brides, this time to North Bay, Ontario. When the train arrived at a drop-off point for one of the brides in the middle of the night, Chase assumed it would be a brief stop. She threw a greatcoat over her pyjamas and added a scarf and a cap. The station master greeted Chase and the bride on the platform, but the bride's Canadian family was nowhere to be seen. Chase went into the station and made a telephone call to the bride's in-laws. As the phone rang and rang, Chase's eyes widened as she saw her train pull away from the station. The station master had waved the train on, assuming her work was done and she was back on board. Instead, she was standing in the station in her pajamas with a helpless bride.

Chase ran onto the platform and yelled at the station master to call the train back. As she stood waiting in the cold, an elderly priest arrived and Chase feared the worst. Thankfully the news wasn't all bad. The bride's in-laws had been in a minor car accident and had asked the priest to pick her up. Everyone's nerves calmed with the news, and Chase's train slowly returned to the station to pick her up. Chase learned a valuable lesson that night: "I never again left a train except in complete uniform."

Margaret Chase was eventually discharged into civilian life with the rank of flight officer in October of 1946, and she married Robert Gibson Sr. on March 1, 1947. She and her husband continued to shop at Beauchamp's until her one hundredth birthday. Her last purchase was a custom-made two-piece grey suit for her centennial. She died on January 19, 2010, at age 104. ⠒

Walter Beauchamp - With my best wishes + gratitude for your friendship over many years -

John B Aird - Lieutenant Governor of Ontario

The official 1983 portrait of the Honourable John Black Aird, the 23rd Lieutenant Governor of Ontario, Canada, wearing the formal uniform tailored for him by Walter Beauchamp. Pictured below it, Aird's personal inscription on the portrait.

The Royal Canadian Naval formal uniform tailored for Captain John Black Aird in September of 1981, one year after he became the 23rd Lieutenant Governor of Ontario.

THE MESS KIT OF MAJOR M. MENDES, AFGHANISTAN, 2009

In the spring of 2009, Terry Beauchamp received an urgent call from the Canadian Armed Forces. A mess kit needed to be altered immediately, and they were counting on him to get it done in time. The reason for the rush was tragic.

Major Michelle Mendes was found dead in her barracks in Kandahar, Afghanistan, on April 23, 2009. She had taken her own life. Her body was being flown back to Canada for a full military funeral. Mendes had been promoted to the rank of major before her deployment to Afghanistan, but her formal mess kit still bore her captain's insignia. It needed to be changed before her burial.

Early on the morning of April 29, two officers from the Department of National Defence arrived at Beauchamp's in an official car and took Major Mendes' mess kit into the shop. They needed it back by the end of the day. Head tailor Alfonso Prezioso (see page 128) put his other work aside, skipped his breaks and meals, and spent the day on the immense task of replacing the braiding on the cuffs and the insignia on the epaulets as well as making alterations throughout the garment. At one point during the alterations, as Alfonso was doing detailed work on the jacket's collar, he called Terry into the workshop. "Smell it," he said, as he held up the jacket to Terry. "You can still smell her perfume."

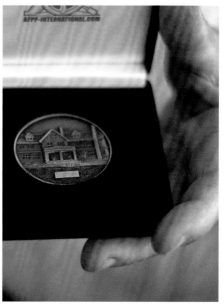

When the officers returned later in the day, the mess kit was ready, and Alfonso received special recognition from the Armed Forces for his efforts—a challenge coin. These coins, a long-standing military tradition, are given to signify a remarkable achievement by members of a regiment or battalion. They are rarely presented to civilians.

A military funeral was held for Major Michelle Mendes on Friday, May 1, 2009, at Sydenham Street United Church in Kingston, Ontario. ⁚⁚

FACING TOP *Major Michelle Mendes.*

BOTTOM *The challenge coin presented to master tailor Alfonso Prezioso by the Canadian Armed Forces for his work in preparing Major Michelle Mendes' mess kit for her burial.*

ABOVE *The body of Major Michelle Mendes returns to Canada, April 26, 2009.*

The Golden Age of Menswear

The two decades between the world wars were a time of great prosperity for Beauchamp & How, despite the economic turmoil of the Great Depression. The company, which had shared space with other tailors in its first decade, took its first step toward industry dominance in 1919 when it took over a double lot at 91 and 93 King Street West, formerly a cigar store. The first floor of the building was used for measuring and fitting customers, the basement for tailoring. Business was so brisk that the company even rented space for an extra workshop down the street at 87 King. With enough

room for a sizable staff of their own, Walter Beauchamp Sr. and Alf How no longer had to rely on outside, piecework tailors. Their success was born of two factors: the tragedy of the First World War and the influence of Walter's wife, Viola (see page 25).

In 1891, the City of Toronto had awarded a thirty-year contract for mass transit to the Toronto Railway Company (TRC), which was owned by Viola's uncle, Sir William Mackenzie. Under that contract, the company was "to institute free transfers, heat the cars in the winter months, uniform all conductors and convert from real horse-power to electric or cable power within three years." And so it was that on August 15, 1892, the first electric streetcar ran up Church Street. Sitting on that car was none other than six-year-old Viola Mackenzie. Horses were soon replaced on every line, and the electric streetcar took over the streets of Toronto. At a time when very few citizens owned a private motor car, streetcars were an essential element of the city's economic health as well as its growth. And the decree that all drivers be uniformed was a boon for Beauchamp & How, as the company had received a contract for uniforms and over-coats soon after it went into business in 1908.

Mackenzie's original contract with the city stated that the TRC would provide service within the city limits. The problem was that between 1891 and 1921 Toronto expanded at a fast pace: from 15,500 to 25,900 acres in area and from 181,216 to 521,893 in population. Powering this growth was the annexation of surrounding villages, such as Leslieville to the east, High Park to the west, and Dovercourt to the north. Even though Mackenzie was willing to build more cars and to improve the downtown routes, he refused to service these outlying areas despite being taken to court numerous times by the city for "inadequate service."

FACING *A view of King Street West decorated for the visit of the Prince of Wales in August 1919. This photo was taken directly in front of Beauchamp & How's store at 97 King Street West, facing west toward York Street.*

ABOVE *This photo, taken on November 28, 1925, shows one of the Toronto Railway Company's old horse-drawn streetcars, which were replaced with electric cars in 1894.*

From The "Climax" System for Cutting Gentlemen's Garments, *published in 1920: a sport jacket and unmatched trousers for a casual look; black tie (in the foreground), with a waistcoat instead of a cummerbund, and white tie (in the background); a double-breasted suit featuring very wide trousers; and a morning coat.*

FACING *A 1923 portrait of a group of Toronto Fire Department inspectors wearing their heavy woolen winter uniforms.*

To fill the void in the outlying areas, a number of transit companies sprouted up, including the Toronto Civic Railways (TCR), the Toronto and York Radial Railway, and the Toronto Suburban Railway. But none of these lines worked in tandem with each other or with the TRC. By 1920, a rider could pay up to nine separate fares to travel from the one end of the city to the other. Though this patchwork system caused consternation for citizens, it was a godsend for Walter Sr. and Alf, who received contracts to provide uniforms for all the railway lines.

It was no surprise, then, that most Torontonians had voted in 1918 for the city to take over the TRC. When Mackenzie's contract expired in 1921, the Toronto Transportation Commission (TTC), which had been created by provincial act a year earlier, was installed to amalgamate the maze of different rail lines under one banner and to move ahead with much-needed repairs and expansion. Along with the consolidated approach to transit, a consignment of red TTC uniforms was required to replace the brown ones of the TRC and the green ones of the TCR, and that task fell to the scissors and needles of Beauchamp & How. This work, along with a contract to make uniforms and overcoats for the Toronto Fire Department throughout the 1920s and '30s, allowed Beauchamp & How not only to survive the economic turmoil of the Depression, but to thrive.

By the early 1930s, however, Toronto's tailors were wringing their hands about a different threat to their industry. The heart of downtown Toronto had shifted solidly to Queen and Yonge Streets with the building of numerous theatres and large department stores, such as Eaton's and Simpson's. And what those stores offered was the greatest threat to King Street's tailors: mass-produced, off-the-rack clothing.

During a speech to a meeting of the Toronto Merchant-Tailors Association (TMTA) in 1931, George Hougham, the head of Ontario's Retail Merchants' Association, told the gathering: "How will the young man whose business you seek know about it? He doesn't even know you are alive. All he knows is that a custom tailor is someone who runs a lot of tapes over a person. 'That may be all right for Dad,' he says, 'but I'm not going to be bothered with that sort of thing.'" Alf How attended that meeting of the TMTA as an executive member (he would go on to become its vice-president in 1937). And what was the TMTA's plan to deal with the spread of ready-to-wear? The status quo, which spelled the end for many custom tailors.

Toronto was as dull as ditchwater in the 1920s and '30s, and was known the world over as conservative and rather puritanical. Ernest Hemingway famously wrote, "I hate to leave Paris for Toronto, the City of Churches." So strict were Toronto's "blue laws," which limited activities on Sundays, that Hemingway had to resort to illegal means to help a friend in need. On his way to visit a friend in hospital on a Sunday, Hemingway stopped in at a druggist's to buy a box of chocolates, only to be told, "We cannot sell candy on Sundays." Instead, Hemingway bought the illicit goods from a bootlegger. Had he been inclined to go tobogganing in any of the city's parks on a Sunday, he would have been forbidden to do so. And, on any day of the week, he could not have gone bare-chested on its beaches. That is, until a sweltering heat wave in 1936, when a group of men rebelled and doffed their woolen shirts. They were all arrested but never convicted. Men's torsos were liberated from then on (women would win the right sixty years later).

This conservatism ran counter to the trends in Britain and America, especially in the 1930s, when the athletic male physique was being celebrated and exaggerated. Sports and outdoor activities were booming; even the comic book hero Superman was born out of this movement. "The emphasis on the sun, on health and hygiene, and on sports activity meant that men wanted to *look* healthy," writes men's style historian

G. Bruce Boyer in *Elegance in an Age of Crisis: Fashions of the 1930s.*

At least when it came to sports, Toronto was in line with the rest of the Western world. Varsity Stadium, on the grounds of the University of Toronto, hosted three separate football teams. Elsewhere in the city, horse racing was thriving and many companies—including the TTC—had their own soccer teams. Baseball was played at the new Bathurst Street stadium, and the Maple Leafs hockey team was born in 1927. The athleticism of the age also inspired Walter Beauchamp Sr. to add a side career. Not only was he an avid sportsman and hunter, but during the 1920s and '30s he became a major boxing and wrestling promoter as well.

The shape of the "new man" was everywhere, and tailors took up the challenge. Inspired by the military uniforms of the First World War, with their cinched and belted waists and shoulders heightened and broadened by epaulets, tailors reinvented the old sack suit of the Victorians and Edwardians. Darts were introduced to shape the jacket around the waist, and padding was added to the shoulders to accentuate them, all to "change the perception of the body beneath the clothes." On Savile Row, the seminal home of men's tailoring in London, tailors introduced extra fabric across the back and chest of the suit jacket to make the body seem more muscular. The resulting waves of fabric looked like curtains, and so the look was called the drape cut. Toronto got its first glimpses of this look thanks to the silver screen—the city was home to dozens of film theatres, and many of Hollywood's leading men wore suits tailored on Savile Row.

The 1930s is widely considered the apex of modern men's style. After the restrictive and drab dress of the Victorians and the Edwardians, but before the grey uniformity that prevailed after the Second World War, the 1930s saw men's fashion express itself as perhaps never before or since. Despite the financial restraints imposed by the Great Depression, the decade was not a time of deprivation in clothing—in contrast to the 1940s, when rationing almost killed three-piece suits and popularized flat-front trousers (leaving out waistcoats and removing pleats saved much-needed fabric). Instead, the biggest change in the 1930s, in contrast to the 1920s, was the subdued palette of colours and patterns.

The wild abandon of the Jazz Age was toned down, with a return to sober greys, muted blues, and subtle patterns. Perhaps this trend was an emotional reaction to the Depression—unemployment had undermined men's self-worth and their role in society. But more likely it was simply an evolution in taste, as English tailors began to be influenced by their Italian counterparts, whose tailoring opted for more fabric, less structure, and a severe v-shape from the shoulder to the waist.

In the United States, young men challenged the norm by wearing blazers and sport jackets in town instead of matching suits, and mixing athletic wear with suits and ties. Button-down collars were worn with ties and tweeds, Fair Isle sweaters, and the more relaxed Ivy League sack suit. As society shifted to a more casual style of dress in the 1930s, and young people, especially university and college students, started to have more influence on fashion, mismatched jackets and trousers became more acceptable. To a certain extent, they were influenced by England's Prince of Wales on his journeys across the pond. Unlike his father, King George v, Prince Edward was a much more casual, relaxed dresser and was regarded as the supreme arbiter of British style. Even so, when the Prince of Wales visited Toronto in the interwar years, the city's tailors were not receptive to his menswear revolution. Instead, they took pride in their traditional and restrained approach to the craft.

Every year at the time, tailors from across North America would gather in Chicago for a meeting of the International Merchant Tailors' Association. The convention included speeches about the state of the industry as well as trend forecasting and a hotly contested fashion competition. Writing about the 1938 convention, the *Globe and Mail* said, "The Toronto delegation will stick to the studied conservatism both in colour and design, a preview of models along Tailors' Row indicated." That delegation included Alf How. The style features that Alf and his contingent from Toronto took to the convention for display included longer coats, pleats, and narrower cuffs, and soft colours as well as midnight blue for formal wear—hardly a menswear revolution. As one of the delegates, R.L. Hewitt, who worked just a few doors down from Beauchamp & How, said, "The Canadian clothes were outstanding at the style show. We have got away from the extreme type of clothes in Canada. We stand between the extremes of the United States and English styles." Consider, of course, that those so-called extreme styles involved slightly more fabric in the chest, or wearing a tweed coat with grey flannel pants.

The Toronto delegation that attended the International Merchant Tailors' Association meeting in Chicago in 1938. From left, Charles Levy, William Given, Alfred How, C.W. Callow, R.L. Hewitt, and George Nyberg.

The waistcoat tailored for Saul A. Silverman in September of 1928. The son of Aaron Silverman, a prominent and successful Sudbury clothier and early Jewish immigrant to Canada, Saul helped establish the Sudbury General Hospital and build Laurentian University. Even though his father ran a large department store, Saul travelled to Toronto for custom clothes.

Though Alf How may not have been a revolutionary tailor, he was a craftsman with discriminating taste—a banker's or a military officer's best friend when it came to custom tailoring. But Beauchamp & How was about to lose his steadying influence at the end of this golden era for menswear. And, as the next decade wore on, the ownership of the company would experience a massive shift. ::

THE FIRST MASTER TAILOR: ALFRED DEANS HOW

Upon his death at age fifty-nine on Saturday, July 6, 1940, the *Toronto Daily Star* called Alf How "one of the best known tailors in Canada." This statement wasn't mere eulogizing. Not only had Alf been a member of the International Custom Cutters' Association of America for many years, but he had also served as its president. The organization, which brought together tailors from across the United States and Canada, met annually to discuss the state of the tailoring industry as well as to provide education and support to tailors; it was a place where they could share and discuss innovative techniques and approaches. In his thirty-two years at Beauchamp & How, he had travelled a number of times to international conferences in the United States, and he had helped establish the company as one of the city's, if not the country's, best-regarded and best-known tailoring shops.

And yet Alf's reputation did not last long in public consciousness after his death. But the How name was reconnected with the history of Canadian popular culture when his daughter, Elizabeth Kathleen, married Foster Hewitt in 1925. Hewitt went on to become the voice of *Hockey Night in Canada*, announcing the first Toronto Maple Leafs game at Maple

Leaf Gardens in 1931 and the first televised hockey game in Canada, between the Maple Leafs and the Montreal Canadiens in 1952.

Relatively late in life, Alf How joined the army, inspired by decades of military tailoring and working with so many soldiers over the years. In 1930, he joined the Irish Regiment of Canada, eventually becoming its paymaster, but he died before seeing active duty. Still, Major How received a full military service, his casket loaded on a gun carriage and accompanied by a guard of honour and a mile-long procession. The daily regimental diaries of the Irish Regiment recorded the event:

July 9, 1940—In the afternoon, 200 other ranks under Major R.C. Rowland, MC paraded to St. George's Church for the funeral of Major A.D. How. All Officers and the Pipe Band attended ... Major How's favourite hymns were sung, "Nearer My God to Thee" and "Abide With Me." The casket was placed on a gun carriage with Major How's sword and Bonnet. The Parade moved off via Queen & University to Mount Pleasant Mausoleum, where the final interment took place. Here the Firing Party fired three volleys, and the Bugles sounded Last Post and Reveille. Thus came to a close the life of a good soldier and a fine man who will be missed by all.

Beauchamp lore holds that Alf How died while working, but the story is only partially true. Alf did suffer a heart attack and collapse while at the tailor shop, but he died at a hospital later that day. In all likelihood, his story became confused with another death that did occur on site. In January 1929, steam presser Morris Teourliou collapsed and died at the company's 91 King Street West location. The coroner determined the death was due to natural causes, even though Teourliou was only thirty years old. ::

ABOVE *The funeral of Major Alfred Deans How on July 9, 1940.*

FACING *The obituary photo of Alf Deans How that ran in the* Toronto Daily Star *on July 8, 1940.*

THE TTC BRIBERY SCANDAL

Walter Beauchamp Sr. was already nervous in January of 1930. Despite the relative optimism of Canadian politicians and bankers, the stock market crash was still fresh in everyone's mind, and Walter Sr. was worried about the effect a recession or even a depression might have on his business. But things were about to get even dicier.

One winter morning, Walter Sr. felt a growing sense of unease as he read a front-page newspaper article about the Toronto Transportation Commission (TTC) and its General Manager, D.W. Harvey, whom he knew personally. A probe was to be held into the commission's operations to examine its alleged malfeasance, including hidden cash reserves, overstaffing, and favouritism in the award of contracts. When he read through the list of companies accused of bribing the commission for contracts, Walter Sr.'s heart skipped a beat. One of them was Beauchamp & How.

Beauchamp & How had been producing transit uniforms since 1908. The company had originally received the contract through Sir William Mackenzie (the uncle of Walter Sr.'s wife, Viola). But Mackenzie's contract had expired in 1921 and he was no longer affiliated with the TTC, so family favouritism had long ceased to be an issue. The complainant was Tip Top Tailors, which had tendered a lower

FACING *A Toronto Transportation Commission streetcar driver in uniform, 1938.*

ABOVE *A Toronto Transportation Commission streetcar driver in uniform, 1939.*

OVERLEAF *A tender between Beauchamp & How and the Toronto Transportation Commission for a consignment of trainmen's overcoats, June 1931.*

TELEPHONE ELGIN 3875

CABLE ADDRESS, BEAUCHA
CODE: 5TH EDITION, A.B.C.

Beauchamp and How Limited

91 King Street West

Toronto

June 2/31

The Chairman,
Toronto Transporation Commission,
Front & Yonge Sts.,
Toronto

Dear Sir:-

   We herewith hand you our tender for Trainmen Uniform Overcoat
as follows:-

           As per sample marked Oxford at $12.50 each
           As per sample marked Warwick at 12.50 each
           4% Sales Tax has been included in these prices

Sample marked Oxford is the same cloth as used for Trainmen's Ov
coats for a number of years with entire satisfaction, and we are
prepared to guarantee it as to wear and fast color.

   We enclose marked cheque for five hundred dollars ($500.00)
being the deposit required by you. Thanking you for past business and trusting to receive this contract, we are

                    Yours truly,

                         Beauchamp & How Limited
                         WNBeauchamp

WNB/GB

price for TTC uniforms but was unsuccessful with its bid, and it remained unconvinced of the commission's impartiality.

So why did Beauchamp & How receive contracts for uniforms when it did not tender the lowest price? "It was on the advice of experts on clothing," said Harvey, during testimony on March 4, 1930. The legal counsel for the TTC asked Harvey point blank: "As far as you were concerned, you had no reason for favouring Beauchamp and How?" Harvey answered no. He claimed that the whole issue had been a mix-up. When Beauchamp & How had sent in its first tender, the sample uniform had been made entirely by hand and thus was quite costly. When the error was discovered, a less expensive machine-made sample was sent as a replacement, and the contract was signed.

One month later, on April 1, 1930, Walter Sr. read the headline in the *Toronto Evening Telegram*: "TTC officials 'honest but too liberal.'" Judge Frank Denton had ruled that in the TTC bribery case, "There has been no appreciable or even discernable evidence of dishonesty in the management of the road, in the form of graft or corruption... [There is] no evidence which reflects discredit on the Commission in connection with ... the purchase of clothing from Beauchamp & How."

His full statement cleared Beauchamp & How of all wrongdoing. ⋮⋮

ABOVE *The front and back views of a Toronto Transportation Commission streetcar driver in uniform, 1952.*

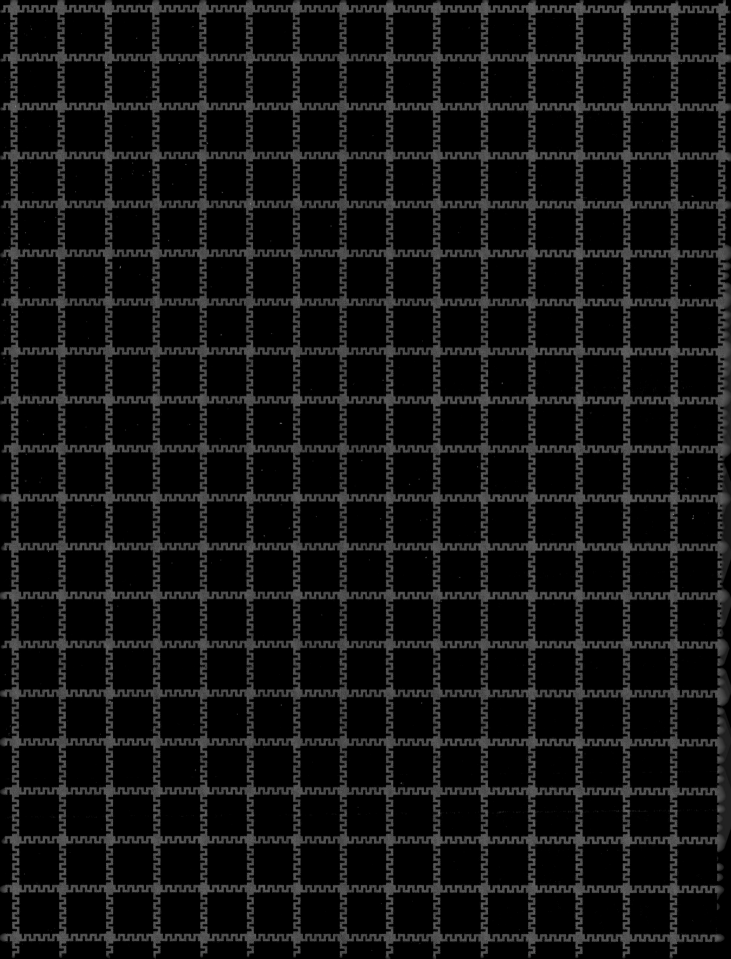

New Ownership in the Mad Men Era

In the summer of 1944, Walter Beauchamp Sr. sold Beauchamp & How to Toronto clothier Samuel Kalles for $43,000. Kalles had immigrated to Canada from Russia as a young man, just a few years before Beauchamp & How was founded. He ran his own clothing company around the corner from Tailors' Row on Adelaide Street and had big plans for Beauchamp & How. Walter Sr. made the sale for several reasons. His partner, Alf How, had died suddenly four years earlier, leaving the running of the business to him. At the age of sixty-three, and nearing retirement, Walter Sr. was ready to relinquish much of the responsibility he was shouldering.

The Second World War also had a major impact on the tailoring industry. More men were choosing off-the-rack garments instead of custom clothing, and margins were getting slimmer—perhaps Walter Sr. felt the winds of change. His son, Walter Beauchamp Jr., was twenty-two at the time of the sale, a fact his grandson Terry believes is the best clue to an understanding of the decision. Walter Sr. felt that he was doing his son a favour. If he sold the business, his son would not have to worry about financial risk but could still have job security, should he choose to stay with the company.

Regardless of Walter Sr.'s reasons for the deal, news of the sale was not made public. Walter Sr. retired quietly to his cottage in

Beaverton while Walter Jr. remained the face of the company and the store's General Manager. Walter Jr.'s presence allowed Sam Kalles to capitalize on the company's name and pedigree and to avoid a costly rebranding. As far as most customers knew, the company was simply handed down from father to son. But the new ownership, as well as the rash of demolitions in Toronto over the next two decades, heralded big changes for the company.

The first came in 1951. After three decades at the western end of Tailors' Row at 91 (and 93) King Street West, Beauchamp & How moved to 77 King West. The western end of Tailors' Row was demolished, a fortuitous development that provided parking for the store's customers. What was most significant was that, forty-three years after its founding, Beauchamp & How took over the most prestigious property on King West. And it further proved its ascendancy by taking over the business of the former tenant, R. Score & Son, which had dominated Toronto's tailoring industry since the nineteenth century.

After the founder's son, Frank Score, died in 1947, the celebrated company had begun to wind down. Sam Kalles bought R. Score & Son in 1951, and Beauchamp & How not only moved into its space but also announced it would "finish and deliver all clothing purchased from Score's." The takeover was complete by 1960, when an advertisement announced that Beauchamp & How was selling Balaclava overcoats, a brand previously owned and developed by Score's.

In the 1950s, Toronto became the economic engine of the country, superseding Montreal. It was also a prosperous time for Beauchamp & How. The company's move to 77 King Street West, its absorption of Score's stock, and its association with Kalles Clothes meant that Beauchamp & How was no longer just a civil and military tailor but, for the first time in its history, a haberdasher. The company now sold everything a man needed for his wardrobe apart from hats and shoes.

FACING A view of Tailors' Row in the 1950s showing Beauchamp & How at 77 King Street West, the former location of R. Score & Son. Dack's is at its original address, 71½ King West. Rogers Jewellers is at 73A (73½), where Beauchamp & How was founded.

ABOVE The first in a series of ads placed by Beauchamp & How announcing the company's move in June 1951. This ad predated the demolition of the western end of Tailors' Row, a site that would become a parking lot for visitors to the company's new store at 77 King Street West.

The Globe and Mail
REPORT ON BUSINESS

TORONTO, TUESDAY, JANUARY 7, 1964

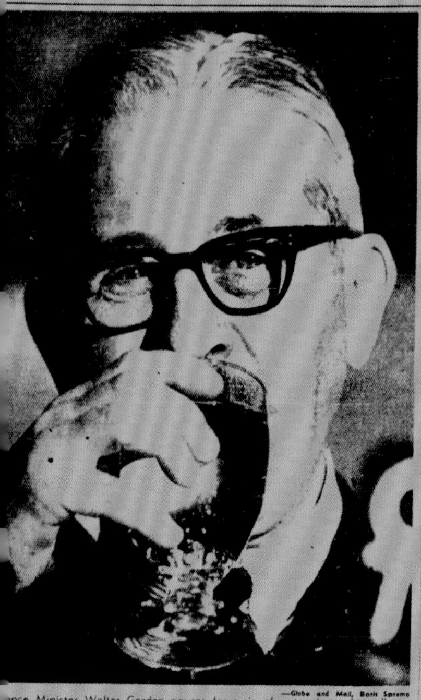

—Globe and Mail, Boris Spremo

...nce Minister Walter Gordon pauses for a sip of water during his talk.

...ed Ink to Keep Flowing, ...nance Minister Asserts

...Minister Walter Gor-...ated yesterday that the ...Government will con-...operate in the red for ...being.

...esent conditions, with ...ment still much too ...get deficits of some size ...inue to be required," he told a luncheon meeting of the Canadian Club of Toronto.

"However, as the economy responds to programs of expansion, Government revenues should increase, some expenditures diminish, and the budget move toward a balance."

The Finance Minister's talk also implied that there was little hope in 1964 for income tax reductions, but indicated that income taxes would not go higher.

"The present upswing in the current business cycle began about three years ago, and one of these days we must expect it to flatten out or take a dip — but a dip that need not necessarily be either sharp or of long duration.

"I mention this as a note of caution, but in the meantime preliminary reports suggest that capital expenditures in 1964 will continue to rise.

See also Looking Into Business on Page B-5

"This will help to support and to expand employment and incomes in all the main sectors of the economy," he said.

Mr. Gordon described current world conditions as favorable for sustained growth in Canada's export markets.

"We probably all feel that President Johnson's veto of the lumber marking bill was a most encouraging sign," Mr. Gordon said in a departure from his prepared text.

The Minister said that greater emphasis was needed in manufacturing to supplement the production of primary industries, and that exports must be increased not only in agricultural products and industrial raw materials but also in some fully manufactured goods.

Mr. Gordon made a brief reference to last June's budget proposal for changes in withholding taxes on dividends payable to non-residents, which he said were designed primarily to introduce a Canadian point of view into the decision-making processes of subsidiary companies that are owned in other countries.

"I expect the shares of many wholly-owned subsidiaries will be made available to Canadians within the next few years," the Minister said — then added, in another departure from his text, "and when I say this let me make it clear that I mean common equity shares of these companies."

In a reference to what he termed the revolution that is going on in Quebec, the Finance Minister gave another indication of the Pearson Government's growing concern over reaction in English-speaking Canada.

"Catching up, especially in the fields of business and finance, is not going to be achieved without incident, without exaggeration, without some intemperate statements being made.

"It is up to all of us to see that this reaction is kept in check," he said.

...ffee Price Raised, ...rease May Be Felt ...Retail Level Soon

...sale price increase of ... a pound for ground ...nounced yesterday by ...Foods Ltd., will bring ...se in retail prices, ac-...o spokesmen for To-...d supermarket chains. ...lers said they expect ...ncreases from other ...nufacturers.

...il price increase will ... mean that a one-...g of Maxwell House ...General Foods brand, ...ase to $1.01 from 97 ...und in Toronto super-...

...Foods also raised its wholesale price for instant coffee by 1 cent an ounce.

The increase follows two other price increases of 2 cents a pound made by most coffee manufacturers in October and November. These were followed by similar retail price increases.

Increase in B.C.

Vancouver (CP) — The wholesale price of ground coffee increased by 4 cents a pound here yesterday, making the cost to retailers 75 cents.

An industry spokesman said a proportionate rise in instant coffee prices may be expected shortly.

...msters Boycott ...ncrete Deliveries

...s construction indus-... face a shortage of ...concrete as a result of ...n by members of the ...al Brotherhood of ... to a new policy by ...ducers governing de-...eady-mix concrete.

...ent-producing firms ... over the delivery of ...ete from the ready-...anies that in the past ...eir own bulk tankers ... cement from the ...

... policy threatens the ...se members of Local ...nternational Brother-...msters who had been ... as drivers of bulk ...wned by ready-mix ...

...**, Teamster** members ...by Canada Building ...efused to accept de-...concrete hauled by ...der contract to the ...ducer.

... official said em-... S. McCord and Co. ...warned they will re-...dle cement brought ...e carriers.

Officials of the two companies declined to comment on the development.

Thomas Lees, president of Local 230 of the Teamsters, said the new policy by the cement firms verges on creation of a combine.

"It's certainly getting away from a free enterprise system when the firms dictate how the cement can be hauled," he said.

Mr. Lees said that the decision of the cement producers to deliver bulk cement would put many small ready-mix haulers in the province out of business.

A letter from one cement company to the ready-mix industry said that after Jan. 1, 1964, all bulk cement shipments would be delivered by contract haulers or by railway hopper cars.

The company said it expected the new policy would contribute to stabilization of prices.

It suggested that customers who wished to dispose of their equipment as a result of the policy change could contact the firm's contract hauler.

Some Operators Jump Gun

Trans-Atlantic Air Fare Cuts Jeopardized as 3 Lines Balk

CPA Fights Bid to Raise Group Rates

By DAVID OANCIA
Globe and Mail Reporter

Montreal—Three carriers may refuse to agree to trans-Atlantic air fare cuts scheduled for April 1 and already announced by some airlines.

Canadian Pacific Airlines, El Al (Israel) and Aerlinte (Eire) have decided to vote against a fare package proposal put forward by a working committee of the International Air Transport Association. IATA cannot announce a fares schedule until there is unanimous agreement of all member carriers.

The three airlines do not oppose air fare cuts. Their opposition is to the desire of some of the major carriers to cut down the volume of low-cost group travel.

News of the opposition to the proposals became known as a major traffic conference of the association got under way in Montreal yesterday.

Many major airlines violated a long-standing tradition during the weekend when they announced their intention to cut fares next April 1 before an IATA announcement of general agreement was made. Among them were Trans-Canada Air Lines, Trans World Airlines, Pan American Airways, British Overseas Airways Corp. and Lufthansa.

The decision of some of the airlines to jump the gun on the announcement appears to be tantamount to an attempt to blackmail the three carriers into accepting the package, group fares and all.

The recommendations were made at a recent meeting in Nassau by the working committee. The results of a vote on the committee's proposals will be announced today.

All of the airlines that decided to break with convention to announce fare cuts before the IATA announcement placed great emphasis on the extent of cuts in excursion, economy and first-class fares. Few made any reference to group fares, an indication of their desire to curtail this end of the business.

CPA, El Al and Aerlinte apparently would like to continue to have the opportunity of developing the group fare system.

The Nassau working group, which recommended sizeable cuts in other classes of travel, suggested that group fares be raised to $328.70 from $312.50 for the Montreal-London round trip, permitting a 21-day stay.

Following are the Montreal-London fares recommended by Nassau working committee's report:

- First class (round trip) cut to $741.60 from $947;
- Economy (round trip) cut to $491 from $507.50 in the 10½-week summer peak season and to $398.70 for the remainder of the year;
- Twenty-one-day excursion (round trip) cut to $299.50 from $355.70;

It is apparent from the above recommendations that those who drafted them wanted to promote travel on 21-day excursion tickets and to cut down group travel. This is precisely what the three airlines that are expected to cast negative votes oppose.

The meeting now under way here is a full-scale traffic conference which has the power to reach agreement on fare structures. It spent most of yesterday discussing round-the-world fare structures and also will consider mid-Atlantic fares during the sessions.

When this particular phase of business is wound up, it is possible that another run will be taken at trying to reach agreement on North Atlantic price schedules to avoid another dramatic fares war such as that which developed last spring when the governments interned.

A-Plan Out, Seeks Hydro In Canada

© New York Times Service

New York — The Consolidated Edison Co. announced yesterday it will drop plans to build a nuclear-powered electrical generating plant in the borough of Queens.

The company said in a statement that it had withdrawn its application to the Atomic Energy Commission for permission to build the plant because it expected to buy large amounts of hydro power from Canadian utilities.

The chairman, Harland C. Forbes, said: "Negotiations with Canadian interests have reached the point where it seems reasonably sure that this is the best way of providing the additional capacity required by 1970 to meet New York City's growing needs for electricity."

Company officials said privately that it was expected that negotiations with the British Newfoundland Corp., a privately owned Canadian utility, would lead to the purchase of about 2,000,000 kilowatts of power from that source. More power may be bought from the Quebec Hydroelectric Commission, a publicly operated body.

The power to be purchased from Canadian sources would be available no later than 1970, Consolidated Edison said, and would be brought to New York on high power transmission lines to be built from the Canadian border to the city.

Mr. Forbes indicated that the much-debated issue of nuclear power use within the city had had not been permanently resolved when he said: "Con Edison continues to look to nuclear energy to supply the additional steam electric power requirements for its system in the years ahead. Our faith in the future of nuclear power in the New York City area remains undiminished."

Opponents of the project had expressed fears about the safety of the use of large amounts of fissionable material in a densely populated area. It is estimated that more than 5,000,000 persons live within five miles of the proposed plant site.

Andrew R. Jones, manager of the preliminary plant engineering section of the atomic power division of the Westinghouse Corp., which was to build the reactor for Consolidated Edison, said in a telephone interview in Pittsburgh: "We are firmly convinced that it would be a very safe device."

British Researchers Crack Egg Problem

The Times of London Service

London — There are more ways of measuring the thickness of an eggshell than by breaking the egg—bending it, for instance.

The Egg Marketing Board, with the resources of its scientific and technical division behind it, has announced discoveries that in any other context might have been styled a breakthrough.

The board has long been sensitive to criticism of eggshell quality. It takes a lot of trouble to measure this so that farmers can find out where their hens are going wrong. Up to now the only methods have been to break the egg and put a micrometer on the fragments or to calculate the shell strength from the force required to break it.

Now scientists find out that they do not have to break the eggs. They simply submit the egg gradually to a pressure of 500 grams, just over one pound, and the amount the shell bends is measured to a thousandth of a millimetre.

The bend is called shell deformation and the board, in a flush of enthusiasm, has made the interim announcement that:

"The investigation, although not complete, does indicate that there is a good correlation between deformation values and shell thickness values."

The board thinks that the new method, less wasteful than the old, will encourage poultrymen to breed hens that lay stronger-shelled eggs. But it has not finished yet. It is expected that scientists will now press on to experiments showing relationships between deformation values and the incidence of damage to the shell.

End Corporation Tax, CMA Urges

Special to The Globe and Mail

Ottawa—Elimination of corporation income taxes and a sharp cut in personal tax rates were recommended yesterday by the Canadian Manufacturers Association in a brief to the Royal Commission on Taxation.

The brief said the fall in tax revenue should be offset by a drastic reduction in government expenditures.

If it were found impossible to cut government spending sufficiently, the CMA said, income taxes should still be reduced, with the short fall in revenues to be made up by a new national sales tax on commodities and services at the consumer level.

See also Ottawa Viewpoint on Page B-5

(The Institute of Chartered Accountants of Ontario early in December made a similar proposal in a brief to the Ontario Committee on Taxation. The accountants called for a single retail sales tax covering nearly all goods and services sold in Canada, with the revenues to be shared by Ottawa and the provinces.)

The CMA said the high level of government spending has placed an onerous burden on most Canadians and on Canadian industry, and that the level of government expenditures, rather than the tax structure itself, is the fundamental cause of public criticism of Canadian taxation.

The brief noted that much of the increase in government spending in the past 30 years had been caused by a few main expenditure programs, including family allowances, old age pensions, unemployment insurance and assistance, hospital insurance, an expanded defense program, and higher grants to junior governments.

"There are good grounds for believing," the brief asserted, "that heavy expenditures in these fields are at the root of our continued federal deficits, our foreign exchange problems and our increasing dependence on foreign capital."

The brief said elimination of corporation income tax, besides ending serious tax discrimination and contributing to a more dynamic economy, would provide a needed incentive for Canadians to invest in equity stock.

As alternatives, if it were not immediately possible to abolish the corporation tax, the CMA recommended elimination of the tax on profits paid to shareholders in the form of dividends, or exemption of dividend income from personal income taxes.

The CMA said its proposed national sales tax, which would ultimately replace federal sales and excise taxes and provincial retail sales taxes, should be shared by Ottawa and the provinces.

The brief urged the federal and provincial governments to reach agreement on what would be a realistic percentage of the national income to be taken in taxes. This figure, the CMA said, should then be considered the maximum limit for taxation in this country.

Pending introduction of the national sales tax, the brief recommended major changes in the Excise Tax Act, which imposes tax on the sale price of goods made in Canada without distinction as to whether the sale is to a wholesaler, retailer or consumer. The brief said statutory authority should be provided for use of a wholesale price in determining sales and excise taxes.

Among other recommendations, the CMA urged:

- Repeal of the sales tax on production machinery, apparatus and parts;
- Sales tax exemption for all articles and materials entering into the cost of manufacturing;
- Permission for corporations to write off for tax purposes up to 100 per cent of the cost of a capital asset in the first year or a period of years at the company's discretion;
- Tax deductibility for the patronage dividends of cooperatives only when such payments are made in cash or its equivalent;
- Substantial broadening of basic exemptions under the Estate Tax Act, together with extension of time for payment of estate taxes.

Juice Substitutes Under Attack, Salada Blames 1962 Freeze

An executive of Salada Foods Ltd. complained yesterday to the company's annual meeting that frost damage to Florida citrus crops in December, 1962, has spawned intense competition from orange juice substitutes.

A. E. Beeby, executive vice-president, said the freeze meant smaller supplies of citrus fruit and higher prices. As a result, he added, promoters and inexperienced operators are beginning to put orange juice substitutes on the market at lower prices than real orange juice.

The substitutes, he charged, "are complete with an assortment of added vitamins which, if they worked, would make Tarzans, or at least marathon runners, out of every man, woman, and child in the country."

Salada is facing extreme competition from marmalades and spreads imported from countries that subsidize sugar, Mr. Beeby said.

Mr. Beeby criticized Canadian advertising and later heard a shareholder complain about some of Salada's own radio advertising.

Advertising perfection often means an unending stream of unimaginative, dull, safe, and sometimes idiotic pale carbon copies of Madison Avenue discards, Mr. Beeby said.

"It is not considered necessary to consider the feeling or intelligence of the audience," he said. "If it were, you would not see those fantastically crude commercials on TV, some of which consist of the owner of the business squatting in a too-small chair, obviously ill at ease, attempting to tell you in a high, squeaky voice about the merits of his next sale."

These advertisers seem to have a disdain for the viewer's intelligence, he added.

Salada aims to give the consumer intelligent, interesting advertising, Mr. Beeby said. Later in the meeting, however, John C. Jackson, retired president of William Shannon Co. Ltd. of Toronto, a textile manufacturer, told the meeting some Salada radio advertising was ridiculous and nonsensical.

Mr. Jackson said after the meeting he referred to a singing commercial spelling out Salada carried weekdays last year at 8 a.m. on a newscast. He said he had heard many businessmen criticize it, and told the meeting he overheard a man in a supermarket forbid his wife to buy Salada products because of it.

Grant Horsey, president, told Mr. Jackson that to be effective the company had to be different. "We make mistakes, but our sales in the past show we have done more good than harm," he said.

Net profit rose in the year ended Sept. 30, 1963, to $2,490,436 or 95 cents a share from $1,425,735 or 56 cents a share the previous year.

Salada sales and earnings were higher in October and November, 1963, first two months of the current fiscal year, than in the same 1962 period, Mr. Horsey said after the meeting. The board of directors was increased to 15 from 13 with the election of L. S. Mackersy, vice-president of North American Life Assurance Co., and Edwin C. McDonald, executive vice-president, Metropolitan Life Insurance Co. of New York.

—Globe and Mail.

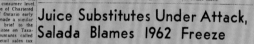

BRICKS FLY AS TORONTO-DOMINION PROJECT BEGINS

Mayor Philip Givens wields sledge hammer to begin site clearing near King and Bay Sts. at the old tailoring shop of Beauchamp and How Ltd. for the Commonwealth's tallest office building. Dominating commercial complex to be developed on six-acre site will be 55 to 60-story head office of the Toronto-Dominion Bank. Allen T. Lombert, president of the bank, is at the mayor's shoulder and at left is E. Leo Kolber of Montreal, vice-president of Cemp Investments Ltd., the company sharing project equally with the bank. At right is Alderman Charles Tidy, grandson of the founder of a flower shop in the block, which will be demolished.

Beauchamp & How had "a well-established reputation as one of Toronto's best-known and best tailors," according to the *Globe and Mail* in September of 1956. The newspaper went on to relate a story that is now company lore: "And with the aplomb to be found only in such an establishment, it was discovered by the proprietors during one heated Ontario election campaign, both Conservative and Liberal leaders were found to be wearing suits tailored by Beauchamp and How."

FACING *The front page of the* Globe and Mail's Report on Business *section on January 7, 1964, featured a photo of then-mayor Philip Givens starting demolition at 77 King Street West. The building formerly occupied by Beauchamp & How was being razed to make way for the Toronto-Dominion Centre.*

ABOVE *The Bank of Toronto building at the corner of Bay and King Streets in 1919. Constructed in 1913, the original building was demolished in 1960 to make way for the Toronto-Dominion Centre.*

OVERLEAF *A 1963 advertisement announcing Beauchamp & How's move to 94 King Street West.*

The building's coming down, we're moving across the street,
and everything must go. Come in and enjoy the healthy savings during the

Made to measure Sale.

As usual, Walter will measure and fit you personally.

BEAUCHAMP & HOW

Civil and Military Tailors
77 KING STREET WEST, TORONTO
(Free parking just a few doors west)

The association with Kalles Clothes and the move to 77 King Street even allowed Beauchamp & How to weather the recession of 1958. When the *Globe and Mail* caught up with Walter Jr. to find out how his company was managing to prosper despite the economic turmoil, he gave the reporter an optimistic statement:

We are feeling a slight falling off in business. Sales are slightly lower than last year but not to a frightening degree. Our customers are not objecting to prices, nor are they short of cash. But since they are generally men in the financial and investment business, they are being rather cautious about spending money at the present time, because of uncertainty evident in the stock market. However, we are not worried: we believe things are going to be fine; and we think it most important that everyone should talk up the state of business rather than spread gloom.

Beauchamp & How's ascendency to the top of Tailors' Row was short lived, however, because of Toronto's voracious appetite for demolition. Philip Givens, the city's mayor from 1963 to 1966, believed that

PREVIOUS PAGE *The old Toronto Star Building (foreground) at 80 King Street West in the 1960s. Beauchamp & How's store at 94 King West was in the row of small buildings to the west of the Star building.*

ABOVE *Curious customers investigating Beauchamp & How's new store in Yorkdale, 1964.*

large development projects were the key to modernizing the city and making its financial sector competitive with the rest of the world. Tearing down old buildings, such as the Corinthian-columned Bank of Toronto at King and Bay, despite the loss of architectural beauty and history, "was considered by many at the time a small price to pay to foster big-city progress," says Toronto historian Adam Levine. It took powerful public campaigns to save a scant few heritage buildings, such as Old City Hall. But the entire block on the south side of King Street from Bay to York was eventually cleared to make way for what was then to be the tallest building in the Commonwealth: the fifty-six-storey Toronto-Dominion Bank Tower. The finished building would be half as tall as the Empire State Building and a symbol of Toronto's economic status. But Walter Jr. still believed in Tailors' Row, even though it was quickly being usurped by the financial sector. "King Street is still the heart of men's tailoring," he said in a 1962 *Toronto Star* interview. "We'll be staying on the block."

In 1963, two years after extensive renovations to its store at 77 King, Beauchamp & How left the south side of the street for the first time in its history. The company moved to much smaller premises at 94 King Street West, next to the original Toronto Star Building. That stunning Art Deco office tower had been built in 1929, with a striking silhouette that inspired Superman co-creator Joe Shuster, who used it as a model for the Daily Planet Building in his comic books. But even a flying superhero could not save the edifice from the relentless demolition of the coming years.

Despite all these moves and the upheaval in the tailoring business, the Kalles family remained ambitious. In 1964, they went so far as to finance a second Beauchamp & How store in the newly opened Yorkdale Shopping Centre. This location stocked ready-to-wear clothes with no production on site, but Terry Beauchamp recalls his father's grumbling about having to "head up to Yorkdale" a few times a week to take orders and look after the shop. Walter Jr.'s daughter, Julie Slater, also remembers his resentment: "Dad would work down on King during the day, take the TTC home, have dinner with us, then drive up to Yorkdale a few nights a week." She believes Walter Jr. resented the Yorkdale store because of the extra work and the nature of the business: "The clientele up there was mostly women shopping for their husbands. It wasn't a men's club like the King Street location."

Sam Kalles died in the summer of 1965, but Walter Beauchamp Jr. had already begun positioning himself to regain family control of the business. Despite his father's best intentions, Walter Jr. was never happy being a mere manager rather than an owner. He often told his family that his father had given him "golden handcuffs": because of his name and connection to the business,

Does *your* suit have this special imported sleeve lining?

(*every suit Walter Beauchamp makes has*)

Who sees the sleeve lining? You do. Your discriminating friends. Your barber. Your doctor (perish the thought). Distinctively striped, hardwearing—yet correct of weight and luxurious in texture—the exclusive lining is one other feature that makes a Beauchamp and How suit the work of art it is. Consider linings such as these as they nestle snugly in a suit created from 8 oz. summer-weight wool. A wisp of cucumber comfort surrounds you as you stroll your elegant way. Coolly, confidently you step forward, because you know Walter has lavished his unique loving care and attention on this—and every garment to leave his establishment. Drop in to Walter's today. Ask to see his sleeve linings.

Are you stifled? Enjoy Walter's care and attention as you consider his wide range of ready for wear, ultra-lightweight wash 'n wear suits—$55—$69. Run the full gamut of summertime wear: inch-trimming Bermudas, light, carefree shirts. And the accessories. Indeed may we say—Walter maketh the complete man.

BEAUCHAMP & HOW
77 KING STREET WEST, TORONTO
(Free parking just a few doors west)

Do *your* trousers have satin pockets like these?

(*every pair Walter Beauchamp makes has*)

Pockets *and* trim, sir. Smooth yet sturdy satin in important regions of wear achieves undreamed of elegance and comfort. Slide your hand into the pocket. Smooth to the touch; firm. Now plunge in recklessly with a fistful of keys and coins; shake well. The seams of this pocket will never part suddenly as you clamber into an XKE or cabin cruiser. Such confidence! you cry. True, sir. It comes from many things. And the fact that at Walter's, every phase of the tailoring operation is carried out in Beauchamp and How's own shop. This means more control, closer attention to detail. Satin pockets and trim are thrown in for good measure. A right goodly measure you'll find a summer suit by Walter from $110.

Wash 'n wear enthusiast? Walter has ready for wear ultra-lightweight wash 'n wear suits — $55 — $69. Trim summer slacks, carefree shirts. And Bermudas — inch-trimming, cool. Stride the fairways in them, lounge elegantly in the quiet of evening. Indeed may we say again: Walter maketh the compleat man.

BEAUCHAMP & HOW
77 KING STREET WEST, TORONTO
(Free parking just a few doors west)

Was *your* suit finished in this old-fashioned way?

(*every suit Walter Beauchamp makes was*)

Egad, Walter's been at country auctions again! No, sir, Walter is posing with the prime finisher of his tailoring establishment —the hand presser. An age-old member of the profession perhaps, but still the only one to impart the truly elegant finish. Walter will use nothing else; notwithstanding the fact that finishing with the hand presser costs him about $3 more per garment than mass-production methods. Impressive? Impressive indeed, sir, when one considers that this and every tailoring operation takes place in Beauchamp & How's own shop. No subcontracting of tailoring chores for Walter. Sub-contracting means to him—loss of control, a wandering of his unique personal attention. He's proud of this oneness of his. And the hand presser. They're both integral parts of Walter Beauchamp's ophelindly.

Are you terribly hot? Take heart. You are never need-lessly so when Walter clothes you. Coolly clad in a ready for wear ultra-lightweight wash 'n wear suit ($55-$69), you're ready for anything. Or the Bermudas, the carefree shirts, the accessories. Indeed Walter maketh the compleat man.

BEAUCHAMP & HOW

Does *your* suit have a special gardenia stem holder?

(*every suit Walter Beauchamp makes has*)

A small point you say? You hate gardenias? Well, tuck a rose or chrysanthemum stem in there. Or flowerless, smile quietly, knowing that this subtle feature is but one of the many that make Beauchamp and How's suits the works of art they are. Look at Walter's loving care, for example. An intangible ingredient, but priceless. He measures each customer with micrometric accuracy. Hovers around the cloth from the first snip of the cutting shears to the final touch of the pressing iron. And presides at the fitting- chalking and pinning dextrously when and if a slight imperfection shows. Order your new mid-weight summer suit from Beauchamp and How. There will be a little piece of Walter's heart in it.

BEAUCHAMP & HOW
77 KING STREET WEST, TORONTO
(Free parking just a few doors west)

he was indentured to work at Beauchamp & How for the rest of his life—but without direct control. So Walter Jr. devised a coup, plotting his insurgency with friend, neighbour, and McCann Erickson ad man Haydn Davies.

Davies' son Trevor remembers being in his bedroom and overhearing many late-night brainstorming sessions fuelled by brandy and cigars. Trevor would hear his father exclaim, "Walter Beauchamp, you're one smart bastard!" Moments later, he'd hear Walter retort, "Haydn Davies, you're one smart bastard!" Their idea was simple: make Walter the face of the company, quite literally. From 1963 on, every Beauchamp & How ad featured the smiling, gregarious face of Walter Jr. The copy often suggested that Walter Jr. *was* Beauchamp & How—it referred to the store as Walter Beauchamp, retaining Beauchamp & How only in the address line—and he was certainly the main reason customers kept coming back.

Despite these moves, the Kalles family would most likely have retained ownership of Beauchamp & How if not for the untimely death of the company's heir, Sam's son Harold "Hershey" Kalles. In August of 1963, Hershey suffered a freak accident during a golf game. As he took a shot from the rough, the head of his club snapped off, hit a tree, and ricocheted back at him. The jagged shaft slashed his throat and he began to bleed profusely. A doctor who was putting nearby ran over and tried to staunch the flow. Hershey was taken to the clubhouse, where a second doctor did his best to control the bleeding. He was rushed to hospital suffering from shock due to acute blood loss and underwent emergency surgery. A few days into his recovery, however, he contracted pneumonia, and two days later he succumbed to respiratory failure at the age of forty-one.

The Kalles family was shattered and decided to leave the clothing business altogether. For Walter Jr., this tragedy was a doorway to his family's future. Reinvigorated by the opportunity to be fully in charge, Walter Jr. made three major changes in 1969: he bought the company back, returning it to family ownership; he closed the Yorkdale store, which had always been a cumbersome distraction; and, most important, he changed the name of the company to Walter Beauchamp Tailors.

Since the death of founder Alf How in 1940, the two Walters, father and son, had employed a variety of tailors. But no one replaced How as master tailor and sartorial

guide until late in the 1960s, when an heir finally appeared. Italian tailor Alfonso Prezioso (see page 128), who had moved to Canada in the mid-1960s, started working at Beauchamp's one day a week, doing a variety of jobs. Even with so few hours in the shop, Alfonso's depth of knowledge and experience were apparent. And when he joined the company full-time in 1970, Alfonso immediately stepped into the role of senior tailor.

The building at 94 King was too cramped for full production, especially with the dozens of suits being ordered every week. Yet the cost of the move to the new address, plus the economic pressures of the time, made it impossible to obtain more space. Therefore, measuring, designing, and fitting were done at Beauchamp's, but cutting and sewing were done by third parties—often one of the city's high-end garment factories. Alfonso ensured that these new manufacturing processes yielded a top-quality suit.

Until Alfonso retired in 2015, his main responsibilities were to measure customers expertly and to manage their fittings. He also recut suits that were already in production, if needed, to be certain of an excellent fit. When a customer came in for a fitting, Alfonso would make sure the garment was being properly constructed. Should any changes be needed to the shoulders, sleeves,

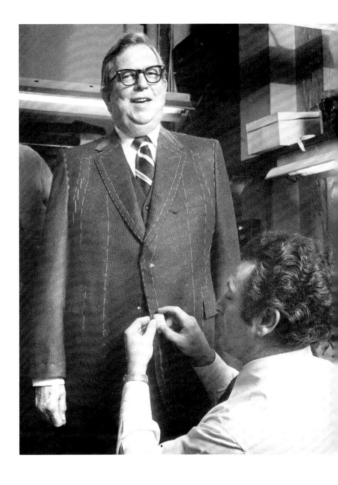

FACING *A mailer announcing the store's move to 18 Adelaide West features Walter Beauchamp Jr., in January 1972.*

ABOVE *Master tailor Alfonso Prezioso marks Walter Beauchamp Jr.'s suit for adjustments, October 1981.*

lapels, and so on, Alfonso would take the garment apart and recut and reshape the fabric to ensure a proper fit. The garment would then return to the factory for the next stage of construction. This detailed, expert guidance set Beauchamp's apart from most of the city's other custom tailors, which had garments made completely off-site and then employed tailors and seamstresses to alter them. And so the rebranded company, back in the hands of the Beauchamp family and employing new staff, was about to enter another stage of prosperity and success.

But the wrecking ball was not yet done with Beauchamp's. When the *Toronto Star* vacated its building at 80 King Street,

adjacent to Walter Beauchamp Tailors, the City of Toronto announced that the entire block, like the south side of King in the decade before, would be razed to make way for a development. The First Bank Building (now First Canadian Place) would take over from its neighbour to the south as Toronto's tallest skyscraper, and Toronto would lose the last remnants of the old King Street.

In 1971, Walter Beauchamp Tailors announced that it was leaving King Street for good and moving into Sam Kalles's old location at 18 Adelaide Street. Even though this chapter of Beauchamp history was coming to a close, another was beginning: the third generation of Beauchamp tailors, Terry, was about to start his career. ::

Starts May 17th
WALTER BEAUCHAMP'S
DEMOLITION SALE

on personally-tailored suits

The Toronto Daily Star building and those adjoining it are coming down.

Walter's stock of suit fabrics must go too — enough for more than a thousand suits, jackets and slacks to be personally-tailored at enormous savings.

Checks, stripes, Glen plaids, solids... lightweights and regular weights; made to your personal taste and with Walter's personal attention.

Come in soon. The jack-hammers are getting closer.

THE DEATH OF WALTER BEAUCHAMP SR.

On Wednesday, July 22, 1953, at age seventy-two, Walter Beauchamp Sr. died of natural causes at his summer home in Beaverton, Ontario. Walter Sr. was born in Toronto and attended Upper Canada College, so we know his family was well-to-do. Although his obituary says he worked for a few years at an importing firm before founding Beauchamp & How, it makes no mention of his first wife, Bessie, or of his careers as a hotelier and a rancher in New Mexico (see page 3). Stranger still, the *Globe and Mail* refers to Walter Sr. as a "noted sportsman." In fact, a number of news articles in the 1920s and '30s referred to him as a boxing and wrestling promoter, but not as a tailor.

Walter Beauchamp Sr. was survived by his daughters, Rosemary and Viola; his son, Walter Jr.; and his wife, Viola. He had spent the decade after the sale of his company away from the city, enjoying a quiet retirement. Though his death left a hole in the Beauchamp clan, Viola ruled the roost until her death in 1977. In the years between the deaths of his parents, Walter Jr. often spent time in Beaverton, receiving support and counsel from his mother. ⁝⁝

FACING *Walter Beauchamp Sr. in the 1930s.*

TOP *Two generations of Beauchamps, 1953: Walter Sr. (seated) and his grandson Terry. (Standing man unknown.)*

ABOVE *The Beauchamp family early in the 1960s. Walter Jr. is in the middle of the back row with his son Terry at his left. Viola Beauchamp (née Mackenzie) sits directly in front of Walter.*

Beauchamp & How

Introduces

A <u>NEW</u> KIND OF CUSTOM TAILORING CONSTRUCTION..

- Shoulders are not excessively wide — yet have a natural square-cut look, regardless of your figure. More rigid construction provides permanency of clean-cut lines.

- Low-set collar adds to the illusion of squareness of shoulder lines . . . enables an impressive proportion of linen to show for good appearance.

- New patented construction eliminates chest ripples and puckering . . . contour remains smooth for the life of the garment. Now, vertical stripes are VERTICAL ALL THE WAY.

- Sleeves taper from fashionable narrow cuffs to full, roomy sleeve heads—Joined smoothly at the shoulder, for flowing lines, achieving a square-shoulder effect.

- Full blade back, combined with higher arm-holes, to enable smooth fit, yet with ample roominess for complete comfort and ease of movement.

- Narrower, straighter lapels, with a much higher gorge line are worthy of particular note. Made with hand-padded hymos for lasting smartness.

Over the past year or so there has been a distinct trend towards a more "natural" cut in men's attire . . . with increasing emphasis on a square-cut shoulder line, without excessive padding. Beauchamp & How designers, after considerable experimentation with lower-set collars, higher arm-holes and high-gorge lapels now feel the desired result has been achieved. We call it our **Grosvenor Square.** Of course, this new style embodies all the custom tailoring niceties for which Beauchamp & How clothes are noted . . . all hand-sewn button-holes . . . hand-stitched edges . . . hand-felled linings. And, as always, full try-ons. We feel that this new **Grosvenor Square** will be enthusiastically received by many of our customers, and invite you to see it.

THE GROSVENOR SQUARE

CHALK STRIPES are once again enjoying great preference —and our fine mill-finished worsteds from Oliver & Jowett lend themselves beautifully to the new **Grosvenor Square.** Available in blues, greys, browns. Priced **$105.**

Beauchamp & How
LIMITED
7,7 KING ST. W. TORONTO
FREE PARKING 2 DOORS WEST OF STORE

BEAUCHAMP & HOW SWINGS INTO THE SIXTIES

Before the Second World War, most menswear advertising in Toronto focused on quality and price. After the war, the word "style" began to appear in advertising copy. Perhaps menswear was entering the modern age of fashion cycles and changing seasonal looks. Maybe returning soldiers wanted to wear clothes that were different from what they, and their fathers, had worn before the war. Or possibly the fast-moving media landscape was focusing on "teenagers" and the young generation. Whatever the reason, Beauchamp & How was not immune to these influences. Instead, it embraced many of them, as noted in a 1961 *Globe and Mail* story: "Three of the oldest men's tailors in the downtown area will be carrying the newest fashion for men: The British Look."

In a rather audacious 1954 advertisement, Beauchamp & How introduced a style of suit called the Grosvenor Square, named for the tony Mayfair area of London. This more modern design represented a sartorial sea change from the bulky, built-up suits of the 1940s to the more naturally shaped suits of the 1950s and '60s. It is remarkable how much tailoring information is included in the ad, suggesting that the men of that era knew far more about lapel shape and shoulder padding than they do now.

Beauchamp & How also appealed to its customers' knowledge when it came to the manufacture of their suits. Undoubtedly reacting to mechanization and the rise of tailoring factories, a 1956 Beauchamp & How advertisement proudly proclaimed: "Every suit custom-made right on the premises!" The company didn't use the word "bespoke" at the time, but it would fit the description: "Every suit individually cut by hand... and with full try-ons." One hallmark of the traditional bespoke approach to suit making is handwork, and a 1963 advertisement states that for all Beauchamp & How suits "Twenty-seven hand operations ensure its being the finest you've ever worn."

But not everyone thought Beauchamp & How was on the cutting edge of fashion. Despite the company's ad campaign promoting the British look, its suits of the time were more inspired by the Ivy League style of America. The Grosvenor Square suit, like the suits Walter Jr. wore in his ads of the 1960s, had natural shoulders and a boxier cut that in fact contrasted sharply with the British style of that era. Lieutenant Colonel Lionel Goffart started ordering

FACING *A 1954 advertisement announcing the new Grosvenor Square cut of custom suits offered by Beauchamp & How. Despite the suit's British name, it is fundamentally American in design, featuring classic Ivy League-style natural shoulders and a boxy, undarted sack fit through the torso.*

suits from Beauchamp's in the mid-1960s, but he recalls wearing a double-breasted suit that had been made at his father's tailor on Savile Row in London. "It reeked of Europe," Goffart said. The built-up shoulders and nipped-in waist were "like a flashing light" on the streets of Toronto.

Beauchamp & How may have become fashion-conscious in the 1950s and 1960s, but it went out of its way to assure Torontonians that the company still held to its founding values. "A conservative firm, Beauchamp and How does not attempt to lead the fashion parade," wrote one *Globe and Mail* journalist in February of 1961. "Some customers have ordered the same type of suit for years, and grandsons to some of the original customers are counted among the store's clients." As men's fashion entered the peacock stage of the late 1960s, with its slim trousers, nipped-in waists, and abundance of colour, one anonymous Beauchamp & How tailor said in a 1966 news article, "We don't cater to that sort of thing in any shape." He agreed, however, that men wanted a touch more panache than they used to, but that Beauchamp & How used colour sparingly and usually confined it to summer jackets, adding, "Our customers are more mature men. We don't go into extreme styles." ∷

Distinguished Civilian Attire Tailored with Military Dash!

Beauchamp and How uniforms have always been recognizable for spirited style and flawless good taste. This style is inherently crafted into our civilian clothing and is highly valued by the younger man as he steps back into business or professional life.

Beauchamp & How
LIMITED

CIVIL AND MILITARY TAILORS   91 KING ST. WEST

FACING *A morning coat tailored by Beauchamp & How in 1954.*

ABOVE *A Beauchamp & How advertisement that ran in the* Toronto Daily Star *on April 13, 1946.*

The young lady—Judy Gammon, will soon be seen as a Playmate of the Month.

bḗ·chŭm or bṓ·chămp?

Your last chance to help. Next Monday Walter Beauchamp
will select the winners of the "Playboy Club" contest.

Walter Beauchamp measures and fits you personally. That is <u>one</u> feature you can get at no other store! Here are some other features of a Beauchamp and How suit.

■ It is measured, cut, tailored and fitted in the Beauchamp and How shop. Most tailors subcontract the cutting and tailoring.

■ You choose your cloth from the bolt — never the swatch. At last count 1194 different materials were on display.

■ The special imported sleeve lining is extra-hard-wearing, extra comfortable, and distinctively striped.

■ Every suit has a gardenia buttonhole and stem holder.

■ Every suit is hand stitched. This helps to retain shape.

■ A hand presser is used on each garment. This costs more than mass production pressing, but the finish is incomparable.

Suits custom-tailored by Walter Beauchamp, from one hundred and ten dollars.

A feeling of suspense hangs over the Beauchamp and How shop. What will the results of the contest be? Be'chum or Bo'champ? Who will win the key to the Playboy Club? The suits? The swords? Will Judy Gammon *really* be Miss October?

One thing is certain, however — and gratifying. Walter's customers *care*. They care about the way they address Walter because *he cares* about how he dresses them.

To understand this sartorial cult, read a little about Beauchamp and How suits for warm weather. Rest assured, sir, this summer you too can be icily immaculate in a suit by Walter Beauchamp —and *how!*

All too recently the principles of the well-dressed man went to pieces when the mercury hit 75°. In despair, he climbed into a shapeless "tropical." No more. The era of the all-wool 8-oz. summer suiting is here.

It keeps its shape as a good worsted will; it "breathes," thanks to its characteristic porosity, keeping you martini-cool in the hottest weather. And it is meticulously made-to-measure as only a Beauchamp and How suit can be.

Why not come in and look? To make it easier to convince yourself, why not use the coupon below as an excuse? It might not arrive in time if it's mailed!

BEAUCHAMP & HOW

Civil and Military Tailors

77 KING STREET WEST, TORONTO

(Free parking just a few doors west)

Dear Walter:
I think most people will want you to pronounce your name:
☐ Bew'champ ☐ Bu'chum ☐ Be'chum ☐ Bo'champ
☐ Smith Other

NAME ....

ADDRESS ....

TELEPHONE ....

The first ten entries selected which correctly forecast the popular choice will become winners of the prizes mentioned above provided the contestants correctly answer a question of skill. Contest closes May 11th, 1963.

THE PLAYBOY CAMPAIGN

Most Toronto newspaper advertisements in the early 1960s were rather subdued. Simple line drawings and illustrations accompanied formally written text that politely invited customers to consider a shop's wares. But in May of 1963, Beauchamp & How broke with tradition and pushed the boundaries of Canadian advertising. Not only did the company use self-deprecating humour and outlandish photography in its ads, it even featured a *Playboy* Playmate, Judy Gammon.

In the spring of 1963, Beauchamp & How launched a contest that played on the confusing pronunciation of the store's name. Customers were asked to vote for the pronunciation of their choice: "Bew'champ," "Bu'chum," "Be'chum," "Bo'champ," or "Smith." The prizes included suits and even military swords. But first prize was racy even for the time—admission to the Playboy Club in New York City. *Playboy* magazine was rather tame early in the 1960s, when it featured far more writing and interviews than nudity, but was still considered too risqué for mixed company. Walter Beauchamp Jr. pushed the envelope further by featuring a *Playboy* Playmate (albeit fully dressed) in the company's advertisements.

The ads were the brainchild of Walter Jr. and Haydn Davies (pictured in one advertisement looking coyly at Gammon). Davies'

son Trevor remembers that Gammon was in Toronto on another project for McCann Erickson, and that Haydn and Walter piggybacked on that visit to arrange for the photo session. The advertising campaign was a huge success.

Even so, Terry Beauchamp and his sister Julie also remember that their mother was not amused. As part of the lead-up to the campaign, Walter Jr. picked Gammon up at the airport and wined and dined her in true 1960s style in advance of the photo shoot. For months, if not years, after the incident, Walter's wife, Elinor, would mock the fluffy little tail worn by *Playboy* Bunnies and call the whole thing "disgusting." Julie thought her mother felt threatened by Gammon, and Terry remembers his mother got so mad that she even threatened divorce.

In the end, though, the audacious ad campaign brought new customers into the store and kick-started an innovative marketing approach that would eventually lead to Walter Jr.'s takeover of the company in 1969. ⁚⁚

FACING *An ad from the risqué Beauchamp & How* Playboy *Playmate campaign of 1963, featuring Playmate Judy Gammon with Walter Beauchamp Jr. and ad man Haydn Davies.*

OVERLEAF *Another ad filled with sexual innuendo for the* Playboy *Playmate campaign of 1963.*

The young lady—Judy Gammón, will soon be seen as a Playmate of the Month.

bē´-chŭm or bō´-chămp?

Everything inanimate in this picture must be won and money besides!

Just advise Walter Beauchamp on how to pronounce his name.

THE FACE OF THE COMPANY: WALTER BEAUCHAMP JR.

Like his father (and his son Terry), Walter Jr. was not a cutter or a needle-and-thread tailor. He was a trained tape man (a measurer and fitter), but more than anything else he *was* Walter Beauchamp Tailors. The company, its brand, and its identity all started and ended with him. Though he may not have wanted to enter the trade as a young man and later in life felt that it had been foisted on him, he did embrace his role and truly made the store his own.

Beauchamp customers from the 1960s remember Walter Jr. as an elegant and supremely courteous man. The shop may have been conservative but it was not snobby, as Judge Donald Dodds, a customer at Beauchamp's since the 1950s, realized when he heard the following story from Walter Jr. The shop was usually patronized by the city's wealthy bankers, lawyers, and politicians, so Walter Jr. was surprised when two railway workers entered the store on a weekday afternoon. The men, in their fifties, were decked out in pristine denim overalls, plaid shirts, pleated, striped railway engineer hats, and heavy leather boots. Though the pair appeared out of place in Beauchamp & How, Walter Jr. treated them, as he did everyone who entered as if, in Dodds' words, "they were company presidents." He showed them

around the shop, introducing them to the custom suits available and the range of haberdashery, but the two men left without making a purchase. The next day they returned in elegant, classically tailored suits. It turned out that they were presidents of two of New York City's largest banks and were in Toronto for a model-railway convention. Both were so impressed with Walter Jr.'s manner, and the clothes on offer at the store, that one of them returned to Toronto for years, expressly to shop at Beauchamp's.

Bryce Douglas, who has been a customer for more than forty years, remembers his first encounter with Walter Jr. back in 1969. Douglas was working as a junior investment banker at Dominion Securities in the Toronto Dominion Bank Tower across the street from Walter Beauchamp Tailors and, indeed, on the site of all the store's former premises. On that fateful day, an impeccably attired senior partner took Douglas aside at work and asked him where he had bought his suit. When Douglas admitted it was ready-made, the partner grimaced and immediately got Walter Jr. on the phone. With Douglas standing awkwardly by, the partner said, "I've got a guy who needs to be tidied up but he doesn't have any money, so make arrangements for him to pay over time and I'll make sure he does."

cool off

When Douglas entered the store, Walter Jr. was hard at work with his jacket off—but still wearing a vest—and with a tape measure dangling around his neck. "We're going to get you some basics," said Walter Jr., picking out bolts of blue and grey cloth. As the tailor laid them out to start discussing styling and features, Douglas summoned the courage to voice his own ideas. "I was thinking of something more stylish…" he began, but Walter immediately cut him off. "No, that's wrong," he declared. "I'd rather you go somewhere else than walk out of here with something inappropriate."

Weeks later, when the Beauchamp suits were ready and Douglas wore one to the

play it cool...

WIN enough ice-cubes for 1000 gin-and-tonics, plus the custom-tailored suit of your choice in **"Walter Beauchamp's Third Annual Contest to Promote the Cause of Lightweight Suitings"**.

office for the first time, his co-workers immediately took notice. "Where'd you get that suit?" one of them asked. "Now you look like a gentleman," commented another. Douglas was pleased, but he hadn't yet paid for the suits and it took him months to do so. Walter didn't mind and was even happy to look the other way if Douglas had to miss a payment or two. When the suits were almost paid off, Douglas wanted to order a couple more. Walter's response? "No more until those are paid for. I don't want you getting in over your head." Douglas wonders whether any business owner would say such a thing today. ::

Custom Tailoring's Last Hurrah

Like his father and his grandfather before him, Terry Beauchamp did not set out to become a tailor. And, like his father, Terry was not forced into the business. Yet it had been part of his everyday life since childhood, and there came a time when Terry started to think that perhaps he could spend his life in the clothing trade.

Just before Christmas of 1971, Terry was on winter break from his business studies at Ryerson Polytechnical Institute and was looking forward to a few weeks' relaxation. Though he'd moved out of his parents' house a few months earlier, he was not surprised when his father called one evening to ask for a favour. A staff member

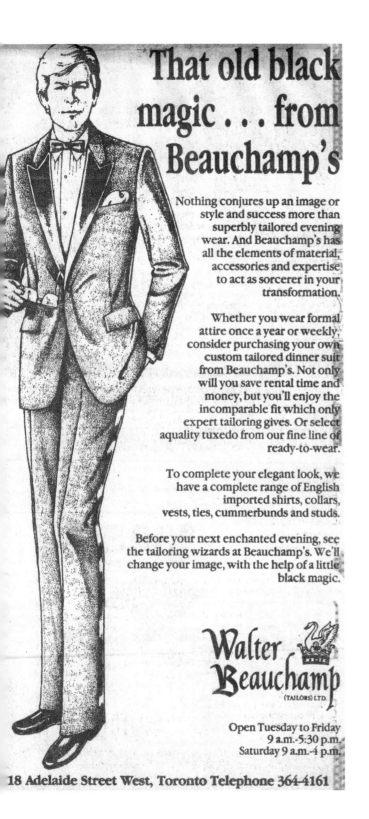
had taken ill at the busiest time of the year, and Walter Jr. said simply, "I could use you at the store." Terry spent the next few weeks taking out the trash, vacuuming the floors, fetching coffee, and doing the dirty work that everyone else was too busy or too specialized for. But from that vantage point—carrying cloth upstairs to the tailors and pressers and then back downstairs to the sales floor of 18 Adelaide West—Terry got an in-depth view of the day-to-day running of a custom tailor's. His interest may have been piqued, but he certainly wasn't ready to commit to a life in the shop.

Two years later, Terry graduated from Ryerson but didn't have a career plan. He worked at a variety of jobs, travelled around Europe, and did many of the things twentysomethings do when they are trying to find their way. But he kept being drawn back to 18 Adelaide, occasionally to help out during busy times but more often because he wanted to be there. Terry wanted to be part of the tailoring world—his father's world—of well-respected and well-dressed men from all walks of life, especially the powerful and the wealthy. Late in 1973, it was Terry who called his father and asked, "Can I come work for you?" And though Walter Jr. didn't hesitate, he made it clear that Terry would have to start at the bottom like everyone else. Terry began full-time as a junior salesman, in the shadow of seasoned and knowledgeable tailors.

Terry wasn't the only Beauchamp to join the company in the 1970s. His brother Bruce also came on board as a junior salesman, though for quite different reasons. During a trip to Europe in 1976, Bruce was diagnosed with pancreatic cancer, and his doctors warned the family that he would need years of gruelling chemotherapy and invasive surgeries to survive. At the time, Bruce was still relatively healthy, and he became an active and key member of the store's staff. But the next decade was an emotional roller coaster for the Beauchamp family, as Bruce descended into poor health, rebounded and returned to work, and then fell ill again as the cancer worsened. When he had to leave work for months at a time to undergo medical treatment, however, he had the full support of his family and never had to worry about losing his job or the roof over his head.

A feature article in the *Globe and Mail* in 1977 discussed why Toronto's older and established merchant tailors were still going strong: "They don't make traditions, they have traditions, and those serve to comfort a clientele that sees no point in changing a good thing." In that same article, Terry affirmed: "The fellows who happen to be our customers have been brought up in the quality of custom clothing and most of them

FACING *This advertisement from October 1986 showcases a remarkably slim silhouette at a time when most suits were Armani-inspired, oversized, and boxy.*

ABOVE *This "Super Spies" mailer from the 1970s was one of the first to feature both Walter Jr. and Terry.*

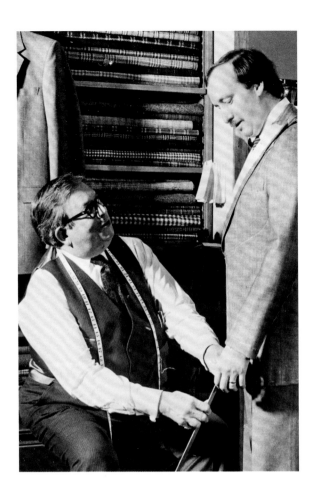

want classic looks, but we're not making the kinds of things their father and grandfathers would have worn." That established clientele—businessmen, lawyers, doctors, professors, and politicians—preferred custom suits from small makers, not off-the-rack clothes from large department stores such as Eaton's and Simpsons (the latter company had quietly dropped the apostrophe from its name in 1972). And it was a clientele, especially in the business world, that was rapidly expanding in disco-era Toronto.

By the time Terry joined Walter Beauchamp Tailors as a full-time employee in the mid-1970s, the core of Toronto had become the Financial District. Where countless tailor shops—including Beauchamp's—had once stood, the Toronto-Dominion Bank Tower (now part of TD Centre), the First Bank Building (later renamed First Canadian Place), and the Royal Bank Plaza had sprung up or were under construction. Sun Life Insurance was building two office towers in the area, adding one million square feet of downtown office space. By the middle of the next decade, about half of Canada's biggest corporations would be headquartered within a few blocks of the place where Beauchamp & How was founded in 1908. Development in the city was pushing farther west and south and included the building of the CN Tower late in the 1970s

and then the remodelling of Queen's Quay Terminal (later Harbourfront Centre), and the construction of Roy Thomson Hall and the Metro Convention Centre (which was kitty-corner to the site where George Beauchamp's hotel had stood 100 years earlier) in the 1980s.

But it wasn't in finance and development alone that Toronto was leading the country. During the 1970s, the city surpassed Montreal as Canada's most populous urban centre. Much of that growth was thanks to immigrants—from Italy initially, but also from China, Portugal, Greece, and the Caribbean—and it ushered in the last great decade of the twentieth century for traditional custom tailoring in Toronto. It was also certainly a fine time for Terry to enter the business.

Walter Jr. was still in his prime, and Terry learned a great deal from him about being a tailor, a businessman, and a leader. He also learned about the importance of grace under pressure. For example, one morning early in the 1970s, Walter Jr. arrived at work only to find his desk strewn with papers and files that had not been there the previous evening. A meek, bespectacled accountant was sitting behind the desk and informed Walter Jr. that he would be auditing the company's books for the rest of the day, if not the rest of the week. "You're at *my* desk," Walter Jr. replied flatly, "and I need to do some work." The auditor nervously gathered up his paperwork and started stuffing it into his briefcase.

Walter turned to Terry and instructed him to take the accountant up to the third-floor stockroom, where there was an extra desk. Terry knew the stockroom well. It contained racks of suits and shelves holding boxes of shirts and ties as well as two large Hoffman boilers that powered the steam presses on the second floor. But he had no recollection of a desk. As the two men entered the room, Terry saw the long work table covered with packaging but it took him a moment to spot an antique wooden school desk tucked away in the corner. Terry politely guided the auditor over to the diminutive writing desk, with its chair attached by a metal bar, and left him to his work.

When Terry got back downstairs, Walter Jr. called in one of the tailors and told him to turn on the boilers. "But, Mr. Beauchamp," the tailor protested, "we don't usually turn those on until after lunch and it's barely ten in the morning." Unfazed, Walter Jr. looked at him and said, "Just put the presses on. I want the presses on." Less than an hour later, a flushed and dishevelled auditor returned to Walter Jr.'s office. With the Hoffman boilers going at full tilt, the temperature in the stockroom had risen to about fifty degrees Celsius. "Things seem to be in order, sir," the accountant declared. "I'll be leaving now."

In his first decade at Beauchamp's, Terry also learned about the intimate relationship that develops between a tailor and a customer—and that it isn't simply a matter of knowing the geography of a customer's body better than the customer himself does. A tailor recognizes that he tailors not only for the body, but also for the customer's vision of himself, whether that vision corresponds to reality or not. Walter Jr. had an uncanny ability to remember all the details of his regular customers and even anticipate their needs, as was evident in the case of Honorary Lieutenant Colonel Edward Arunah Dunlop Jr.

Dunlop was a Member of Provincial Parliament (MPP) in the 1960s and a Cabinet Minister under Ontario Premier William "Bill" Davis. He was also the founding National Director of the Canadian Arthritis and Rheumatism Society as well as the first President of the *Toronto Sun* newspaper. His tailoring standards were exacting because of his prominent positions in society. Equally challenging was the fact that Dunlop was blind.

During a training exercise with the Queen's Own Rifles of Canada in September 1944, Dunlop, a Major at the time, had been instructing junior soldiers in how to throw grenades. One of the soldiers dropped a live grenade; Major Dunlop attempted to dispose of it, only to have it explode in his left hand, severing fingers and leaving him blind in

The Honourable Pauline Mills McGibbon was Ontario's 22nd Lieutenant Governor, from 1974 through 1980. She was not only the province's first female Lieutenant Governor, she was also the first female Viceregal Representative. She is pictured here with her husband Donald on December 19, 1986, in blazers that were tailored by Walter Beauchamp and feature the standard of the Lieutenant Governor of Ontario on the breast pockets.

both eyes. Walter Jr. had been tailoring for him since that time and seemed to know instinctively what he needed.

When Dunlop visited the shop to order a suit, Terry would often sit off to the side, watching his father in action. Walter Jr. knew, from a simple description such as "a broad stripe, not a pin stripe" or, simply, "blue," the exact fabric that was wanted. Terry always wondered how his father did this, but Walter Jr. would just say confidently, "Terry, I know what Colonel Dunlop needs."

Terry recalls prominent customers who bought custom-made and off-the-rack garments from Beauchamp's in the 1970s and early in the '80s, including members of the Eaton family, then–prime ministers Joe Clark and John Turner, Toronto mayors David Crombie and John Sewell (who was introduced to the store by his father, long-time customer Bill Sewell), Aboriginal leader Phil Fontaine, as well as lawyer and activist Clayton Ruby. And yet, in the midst of this boom, change was afoot in the tailoring industry. Even though the city still had its fair share of custom tailors, the big names started to disappear, shutting their doors for

FACING *A green velvet smoking jacket, with a black grosgrain shawl collar, that was tailored for Colonel Edward Dunlop by Walter Beauchamp in 1975.*

ABOVE *A multicoloured striped suit that was tailored for Colonel Edward Dunlop by Walter Beauchamp in 1973.*

ABOVE LEFT *Merton Chesher and "Colonel" Harland Sanders, 1969.*

RIGHT *The men of Beauchamp's in a photo taken for the mailer campaign of Christmas 1981, featuring Bruce and Walter, Terry (seated), and Terry's first son, Craig, sitting on his lap.*

FACING *Tailor Louis Ruben standing in front of his shop at 248 Royce Avenue (now 1558 Dupont Street), ca. 1944.*

good because of retirement or impossibly high rent increases caused by the real estate boom. Three of the biggest names in Toronto tailoring in that era—Skitch Clothes, Louis Ruben, and Merton Chesher—all migrated to Beauchamp's.

Skitch Clothes Ltd. was founded in Toronto in the 1830s and was owned by Tudor Harries in the late 1970s. When Harries decided to retire, Walter Jr. worked out an arrangement with him whereby Skitch customers were encouraged to switch to Beauchamp's, with Harries helping the

transition in the early months. He set up a similar arrangement with Merton Chesher, who had helped conceive, as well as tailor, the double-breasted white flannel suits worn by "Colonel" Harland Sanders, the founder of Kentucky Fried Chicken. In September of 1980, Chesher closed his shop on Richmond Street and continued to serve his former customers at Beauchamp's on Adelaide three days a week. As a part owner of Scott's Chicken Villa (the Canadian wing, so to speak, of Kentucky Fried Chicken), Chesher connected Beauchamp's to the iconic chicken chain. For the next decade, Walter Jr. and his staff provided bolo ties to Scott's staff across the country.

The event that had the most impact on Beauchamp's during the 1980s, however, was the closure of Louis Ruben, founded many decades earlier on Royce Avenue (which later became Dupont Street). The original tailoring company had been passed down to the founder's sons, Max and Gordon, when Louis died in 1970. Max was the tailor and Gordon was a salesman. When Max died late in the 1970s,

Gordon was unable to continue running the company. But, instead of simply selling his customer list to Walter Jr., Gordon moved to Beauchamp's and worked as a full-time salesman with the company for two decades. During his time at Beauchamp's, Gordon continued to offer his customers some special services, including his signature single-button cuff (which annoyed head tailor Alfonso because such a button generally connotes casual attire) and the original "Louis Ruben" tags on the inside of jackets. Walter Jr. initially turned a blind eye to this practice, but Terry put an end to it late in the 1980s.

In that decade, urban development was still in high gear in the city. Beauchamp's had already moved five times since its founding to escape the wrecker's ball and it wasn't finished yet. Walter Jr. had heard whispers among his customers about a plan for a development on Adelaide, just west of Yonge. Sensing an opportunity and recognizing his diminishing health, Walter Jr. sold the building at 18 Adelaide to a group of developers in 1984 with an agreement that Beauchamp's would continue to rent its space for another three years until the company was ready to move. This arrangement turned out to be a better

deal for Walter Jr. than for the developers. Owing to a recession late in the 1980s, construction of the Bay Adelaide Centre became a stop-and-go proposition. The first phase, the west tower, was finally completed in 2009; but tenants are only now moving into the east tower as this book goes to print, nearly thirty years later.

Terry took over the operation of the company just as Beauchamp's needed to find a new home. Walter Jr.'s health was declining, as was that of Terry's brother Bruce. At first, Terry wanted to relocate just east of Yonge Street, perhaps to Toronto Street, which was close to the company's former

FACING *The staff of Walter Beauchamp Tailors, ca. 1983. From left, Walter Jr., Tim Heflin, Terry Beauchamp (in front), Bruce Beauchamp, Alfonso Prezioso, and Gordon Ruben.*

ABOVE *The store at 18 Adelaide Street West early in the 1980s. Dack's was a neighbour of Beauchamp's from its first days on Tailors' Row on King Street West through to its Wellington Street location.*

OVERLEAF *An April 1989 advertisement announcing the arrival of Walter Beauchamp Tailors' new neighbour, SkyDome. The first baseball game was played in the SkyDome to a crowd of more than 48,000, five times as many fans as had joined Walter Beauchamp Sr. on the Toronto Islands to watch the Maple Leafs baseball team eight decades earlier (see page 20). Sadly, the Blue Jays lost their opener to the Milwaukee Brewers.*

Your new Beauchamp's suit could put you in the SkyDome for the Gala Opening

locations and existing clientele. But Ken Jones, a Ryerson professor who specialized in retail location (and later became Dean of the Ted Rogers School of Management), whom Terry had met through a neighbour, immediately advised against it. Jones argued that a dividing line ran along Yonge in the downtown core. In the area east of Yonge were churches, hospitals, and Ryerson Polytechnic Institute, which meant that it wasn't a business environment but a zone of transition. Most important, there were no

offices in the area because, at the time, it was not on City Hall's redevelopment agenda.

The area that *was* in the city's development crosshairs, however, was just west of University Avenue as well as in the south end of the city. Jones recognized that rapid growth, sparked by the opening of Roy Thomson Hall in 1982 and the Metro Toronto Convention Centre in 1984, would continue. SkyDome (now Rogers Centre), which opened in 1989, and the new headquarters of the Canadian Broadcasting

Centre, which opened in 1992, were already in the works. Most important, as Jones pointed out, a location west of University and south of King—in other words, in the Front Street area—was only a ten- to fifteen-minute walk to the financial hub of the city at Bay and King. By that time Beauchamp's had become a destination that customers sought out as opposed to just wandering into, and Terry wanted the store to be conveniently situated.

Terry decided to take Jones's advice. At the corner of Wellington and Simcoe Streets, he found large ground-level premises that offered plenty of visibility, room for all his stock, and space for five or six alterations tailors. Terry could even rent out part of the premises to Dack's, the footwear company that was his neighbour on Adelaide (as it had been through all of Beauchamp's years on King Street). But Walter Jr. was

skeptical. "Why would you go there?" he asked Terry in the summer of 1987. "There's nobody down there." Terry tried to assure Walter that within a decade fifty thousand people would be living on their doorstep. "Where will they live?" asked Walter. "In the parking lots?" Having spent his whole life in Toronto, Walter simply couldn't believe that people would ever want to live and work near the old rail yards. Walter finally acquiesced: "For your own sake, I hope you're making the right decision." So, in October of 1987, Walter Beauchamp Tailors moved to 145 Wellington Street West. It would become the company's home for nearly thirty years— its second-longest spell at any location.

The first few years on Wellington were challenging. The store's relative isolation meant that sales were slow. And the recession didn't help. But it was Bruce Beauchamp's death on April 18, 1988, that

Hook Into Terry's Summer Suit Contest

Tally-Ho!
IT'S THE BEAUCHAMP
FOUR DAY EVENT.
GOOD HUNTING!

put all those concerns in perspective. Even though the family had expected Bruce's death for years, losing the baby of the family crushed Walter's spirit. He didn't reveal his grief, being from a generation of men brought up to keep their emotions to themselves, but he retreated from the day-to-day operation of the store. Terry and Bruce had run the company jointly through most of the 1980s, with Bruce doing as much as he could between his bouts of illness. But, with Bruce gone and Walter Jr. retired, Terry started the decade fully in charge, the third Beauchamp to oversee the family legacy.

Business picked up for Beauchamp's, and the company was producing dozens of suits a week by the late 1990s, but this success papered over a worrying trend in menswear. Increasingly, companies no longer required that employees wear a suit in the office and, thanks to Casual Fridays, suits were disappearing completely from some men's closets. Less expensive off-the-rack and designer clothes put pressure on custom tailors, as more men opted for ready-made rather than custom-fit clothing. Yet Beauchamp's just got busier.

The company's continued success was the result of two factors. First, Terry had added a fair amount of high-quality casual clothing into the store's haberdashery. That way, when CEOs stopped buying custom

Together again, Toronto's best-dressed couple

Dack's Shoes and Walter Beauchamp Tailors are back together again at their new location, kitty corner to Roy Thomson Hall, at Wellington and Simcoe Streets.

For over 60 years, at two previous locations, Dack's and Beauchamp's have offered Toronto's most discerning men, the convenience of being impeccably dressed from head to toe at one central location.

Take part in a continuing tradition of excellence by visiting their new location today.

Dack's SHOES

Agents for

Church's
famous English shoes

53 Simcoe Street,
Toronto

977-3915

Walter Beauchamp (TAILORS LTD)

145 Wellington
Street West,
Toronto

595-5454

suits, they would still come in for casual jackets and trousers. Terry made sure that his merchandise, though ready-made, reflected Beauchamp's quality and style. Walter Jr. had advised him to avoid well-known brands, items that customers could find easily in other shops. "The only thing that is unique to us," he would say, "is us." People wanted to buy Walter Beauchamp— an approach to style and wardrobe—not just clothes. Or, as Walter Jr. said, "If they're buying Walter Beauchamp, then you'll have a customer for life."

Second, the number of custom tailors in Toronto was shrinking. Many of the city's established tailoring houses, including Ed Provan, Cameron & Jeffries, Alan Ely, Frank Flanagan, the Lloyd Brothers, Bigelow & Beattie, and Bill Griner, shuttered their businesses by the end of the 1990s. With all these tailors disappearing, many of their customers migrated to Beauchamp's, increasing its share of the market even though that market was declining at an alarming rate.

Throughout the 1990s, Walter Jr. would still visit the shop on occasion, though his severe arthritis made walking difficult. When Walter's wife, Elinor, suffered a heart attack early in the 1990s, she could no longer care for Walter and he moved into a nursing home. Then he had a severe stroke. As Terry

sat by his father's bedside, he reminisced about everything Walter had taught him, as a father and as a businessman. Walter Jr. had a way with people and a fantastic sense of humour. He was lovable, but you never wanted to cross him. Most important was his integrity, which he instilled in his family and co-workers. "If you never make mistakes," Walter often told his son, "then you're not doing anything."

Walter "Sonny" Beauchamp died on August 25, 2001. Out of respect, Terry closed the store for three days of mourning and commemoration. When the store reopened, the staff were overwhelmed with letters and visits of condolence in the following weeks. Not only had a beloved tailor died—a man known across the city and the country, inside and outside the industry—but a connection to old Toronto had been severed. ::

MASTER TAILOR
ALFONSO PREZIOSO

Alfonso Prezioso was born into a family of tailors in a small village near Naples, Italy, in 1938. The tradition reached back to his grandfather. Alfonso's uncle Giuseppe was regarded as one of Naples' finest tailors, who were known for soft construction that used little or no padding to create a jacket light enough for the hot Italian summers. When Alfonso was eight years old, he began to apprentice under his uncle, doing menial tasks and spending tedious sessions learning the basics of hand sewing. Alfonso attended tailoring school as a teenager to learn pattern making and design, and then completed a year of military service. But, instead of training to be a soldier, he was directed to put his superior tailoring skills to work mending and altering uniforms, as well as making garments for officers.

Alfonso left the army in the 1950s and opened his own tailoring shop in Prato, a small town outside Florence, expecting to spend his life there. But Alfonso's brother-in-law, also named Giuseppe, had moved to Toronto and saw a city full of opportunity. He convinced Alfonso's wife, Angela, that they would do better in Canada and that it was an ideal place to raise a family. In 1964, Alfonso sold his shop and all his tailoring equipment and the family moved to Canada.

Despite the massive change the Preziosos had just made, Angela was not a risk taker. She encouraged Alfonso to settle down quickly and find a job instead of opening his own shop again. At first, he tried working at a garment factory but discovered that his talents were wasted. It took a few years, but eventually he made contact with Walter Beauchamp Jr. and started working for the company part-time in 1968. Alfonso impressed Walter with his immense skill and knowledge of hand tailoring, and in 1970, a few months before the store moved to Adelaide Street, Alfonso joined the company as Senior Tailor. It was a position he would hold until his retirement forty-five years later, in 2015. ⁚⁚

THE BRUCE BEAUCHAMP
MEMORIAL FUND

On the day that Bruce Beauchamp died in 1988, Walter Jr. resolved to make something positive of the tragedy. Bruce had many friends and relatives across the city, the country, and the world. Walter knew there would be a massive outpouring of love and support, so he gathered the family and proposed an idea. "Instead of so much money being spent on flowers, we should do some good in the world." And so the Bruce Beauchamp Memorial Fund was created.

Walter and his wife Elinor got the fund going, but it grew quickly with the help of family and friends. Terry and his wife Helen, along with Terry's sister Julie Slater, look after the daily management and absorb the administrative costs so that all the money raised can be donated. The fund supports a variety of health care causes, including the Princess Margaret Cancer Foundation and the Centre for Addiction and Mental Health Foundation. Bruce's spirit lives on through the fund, and Terry says that looking after the fund makes him feel that Bruce is still with him and that he's working on Bruce's behalf, even today. ::

FACING *Master tailor Alfonso Prezioso in the mid-2000s at the Wellington Street store.*

TOP *Bruce Beauchamp late in the 1970s.*

MIDDLE *Terry and Bruce Beauchamp unpacking neckties for display in the store at 18 Adelaide Street, ca. 1985.*

BOTTOM *Walter Beauchamp Jr. and Terry in the Adelaide Street store in the mid-1970s.*

COURTLAND PARFET AND THE RHINOS OF KENYA

Soon after the store moved to Wellington Street, a new customer caught Terry's eye. The man appeared to have just stepped out of an English country home: he was wearing a hacking jacket and an ascot, and his manner reminded Terry of the actor William Holden. The man didn't say much; he just browsed through the shop and then left. But he returned the next day, and the day after, each time silently browsing the merchandise. After about a week of this, the man finally asked Terry whether he would repair a loose button on his jacket. While the button was being reattached, Terry tried to find out more about the enigmatic man, but the most he could elicit was "I'm not from around here."

A week later the man returned, ready to reveal his identity and order some clothes. He was Courtland Parfet, a former mining magnate who owned Hollywood Chewing Gum as well as Solio Ranch, Kenya's largest tract of private land, which had one purpose: to save the endangered rhinos of East Africa.

Parfet had originally visited Kenya in the 1950s to hunt rhino. He purchased Solio in the late 1960s, but after finding the body of a poached rhino in 1970—the last one indigenous to the area—he converted the estate to a conservation area. Inspired by his wife, famed wildlife photographer Claude Parfet, he never hunted again. Instead, he became a champion of black rhinos. The remaining wild rhinos of Kenya were gathered and moved to the sanctuary, where Parfet and his wife worked tirelessly for decades to protect them from poachers. Today, the ranch is recognized for having saved from extinction not only Kenya's black rhinos but also its white rhinos.

Terry was humbled by such a commitment to conservation and also pleasantly surprised when Parfet decided to order some custom clothes from him. Parfet was in Toronto for an extended visit while his wife underwent treatment in a local hospital. Over the next few months, he ordered a number of classically styled sport jackets and trousers. Parfet was so impressed with the garments and the service that he kept ordering from Beauchamp's, even after he returned to Kenya. For years after this initial "courtship," Parfet would call Terry from Africa to order more clothes. With measurements in hand from Parfet's previous fittings, Terry would make the garments in Toronto and ship them to Kenya.

Some years later, Terry happened to watch a documentary about Parfet's conservation work at the ranch. It was an absorbing tale, but what gave Terry extra pleasure was that, in the film, Parfet wore a jacket made by Beauchamp's. ⠒

FACING *Courtland and Claude Parfet feed a black rhino on their Solio Ranch in Kenya, 1980s.*

Walter Beauchamp's Reborn

Early in the 2000s, the city of Toronto was both blossoming and struggling. An outbreak of severe acute respiratory syndrome (SARS) in 2003 threatened to quarantine the city for months. Although that did not happen, the mere possibility sent the city's economy into a tailspin. Hotels lost millions of dollars from cancelled reservations, restaurants saw bookings drop as much as 30 percent, and theatre audiences shrank drastically.

But that year also witnessed the opening of the Distillery District, a rare example of Toronto's not only recognizing its history,

but also celebrating it. The transformation of a derelict, 150-year-old whisky distillery into a thriving commercial and residential area allowed the city to save more than just North America's largest collection of Victorian industrial architecture. The Distillery District proves what historically minded Torontonians have been saying for decades: history is a huge, untapped resource worth preserving.

As Toronto wrestled with change at the dawn of the twenty-first century, so, too, did the clothing industry. Until late in the 1990s, business at Beauchamp's had steadily increased or remained stable year over year, and sales were predictable. But then sales began to fluctuate dramatically: one year the store would be relatively successful, the next it would incur losses. The dress-down movement of the 1990s had infiltrated the business world, if not society at large; but Beauchamp's was a small company serving a niche clientele and it was better equipped to weather the storm in the menswear industry than were most of its competitors. Thanks to its high-end haberdashery and strong custom-tailoring clientele, Beauchamp's was able to balance its sales The bigger threat was the Internet. Terry could see the impact of this borderless business on his store almost every day. People would go into Beauchamp's, try on ready-to-wear, and nonchalantly admit they were testing sizes before buying the same product on-line, and

at a much lower price. The future of custom tailoring was looking bleak.

And then something wholly unexpected happened: *Mad Men.* In 2007, in an age when fewer people were watching cable TV, the program's dark take on the Manhattan advertising world as it represented the American Dream of the 1960s—a shiny suburban world of artificiality, rife with sexism and fuelled by cigarettes and alcohol—became required viewing. But it was also a constant reminder that suits look sharp. The show played into the anxieties of a male generation for which there was no clear definition of manhood. The suits of *Mad Men* reflected a time when men were grown-ups and boys were children,

and they dressed accordingly. It was a far cry from the baseball caps, sneakers, and T-shirts that had become popular with all ages and were worn in virtually all settings. *Mad Men* inspired a revival of the slim-fitting Sixties suit, even though most of the men who embraced this trend were unaware of the social psychology behind the style they were adopting.

FACING *Toronto's Distillery District in 2012. The area was originally occupied by Gooderham & Worts Limited, the largest distiller of alcohol in Canada. The descendants of the founder, William Gooderham, were long-time Beauchamp & How customers.*

ABOVE *The cast of* Mad Men, *2009.*

Beauchamp & How had made these Sixties styles of clothing during the original Mad Men era, just as it had long ago made the type of clothes worn on the hit series *Downton Abbey*, set in post-Edwardian Britain. The tailors of Beauchamp's had watched the frock coat give way to the sack suit and the drape cut of the 1940s, and finally to the slim suits of the 1950s and '60s. Beauchamp's was tailoring clothes throughout each of those eras, creating and making the clothing styles that people wore daily, and that were now being celebrated in contemporary movies and television.

Those who wanted slim, overtight suits were predominantly young men who embraced trends and fashion. They wanted a look that was classic yet distinct from what their fathers wore. Beauchamp's did offer such styles, but the company has never been a fashion brand, and outright trendiness is not in its DNA. As its tailors and salesmen had stated decade after decade, they "didn't go in for all that." Beauchamp's made contemporary clothing with a single motivation: to create traditional, conservative suits of quality for a powerful and influential clientele. Despite occasional requests for "costume uniforms" or flamboyant capes, most of Beauchamp's creations weren't designed to attract attention or to draw the eye. Proportions, patterns, and cuts were classic and moderate. Beauchamp's provided suits that fit the individuals who wore them. And so the *Mad Men*-inspired craze of slim suits hardly touched the shears and needles of its tailors.

Despite the renewed interest in suits, the corporate world that Beauchamp's served was still on a slide toward casual wear. And so the business continued to be unstable and unpredictable. Even so, at Walter Beauchamp Tailors, positivity prevailed. Amid the harsh realities of a changing menswear culture, the advent of on-line shopping, and cut-rate overseas custom tailoring, in the 2000s the company saw one of its most famous and important customers step through its doors.

Singer-songwriter Gordon Lightfoot was supposed to have visited Walter Beauchamp back in the mid-1980s. Howie Freeman, who was a friend of Lightfoot's and had worked with Gordon Ruben, called Beauchamp's to say that Lightfoot needed some clothes and would be visiting the store. Terry, Walter Jr., and the staff waited, but Lightfoot never arrived.

Twenty years later, in 2003, Freeman called the store again. Lightfoot had recently fought a serious illness that had put him in a coma for six weeks. He was recovering and was planning to go back on tour. Lightfoot again needed clothes, but this time Terry didn't hold his breath. So Terry was shocked and excited a few days later when he received a call from Lightfoot's sister Beverley, who invited him to Gordon's house for a personal consultation. When Terry arrived and knocked at the door, he expected to be greeted by an assistant or perhaps by Beverley herself. "You're the tailor?" said Gordon Lightfoot as he stood on the other side of the open door. Terry nodded. "Good," he continued, inviting Terry in. "I'm going on another tour and I need some things altered."

Strictly speaking, Beauchamp's had never been an alterations shop. Then again, it was Gordon Lightfoot who was asking for the alterations. Terry didn't balk, even when Lightfoot brought out the first garment that needed adjusting. It wasn't a jacket or a waistcoat, not even a pair of dress pants. He wanted an old pair of Levi's jeans let out at the waist. With his father's resolve, Terry didn't blink an eye but assured Lightfoot that the job would be done expertly.

Back at the shop, Terry, Alfonso, and sales associate Bob Kane contemplated the jeans in dismay. Unlike custom clothes, jeans have no extra fabric to facilitate an alteration of this nature. And the jeans were of such a specific style and age that new denim couldn't be swapped in. The next day, Bob showed up at work with an identical pair of jeans from his own wardrobe. "Rip 'em apart, if you need to," he told Terry, for he too had learned from Walter Jr. that the show must go on. In the end, Bob's jeans were cannibalized, Gordon Lightfoot was delighted, and a relationship was begun.

Over the next several years, Beauchamp's would go from altering Lightfoot's garments to making him custom-tailored waistcoats, jackets, and trousers, many of which he wore on tour. Though he had performed a few times since his illness, he finally announced a concert tour in 2005. Before his return to the stage in Toronto, he arrived unannounced one morning at Beauchamp's and asked the staff to join him in the fitting area. When everyone was assembled, he handed each staff member an autographed ticket to the first of his four shows at Massey Hall, only steps from the shop. During the concert, Lightfoot gave emotional thanks to everyone who had helped him overcome his illness and resume touring—and he singled out "all the people at Walter Beauchamp Tailors."

In the summer of 2013, Pedro Mendes was working as a radio producer at the Canadian Broadcasting Corporation. He had pitched an idea to his senior producer for a documentary about tailoring. Even though he was working a block away from Beauchamp's, he had never entered the shop. Then one day, as he walked past, he noticed that just under the "Walter Beauchamp" sign was a small inscription that read "1908." He was intrigued, walked in, and made the rookie mistake of asking to speak with "Mr. Bo-SHAW." Mary McGuigan, who managed the store, politely corrected him and then called Terry from the back office.

As Pedro recalled, " Terry wasn't sure that a radio documentary could truly convey what tailoring involves, but he humoured me. Over the next few months, as I documented the process of getting my first custom-tailored Beauchamp suit, Terry treated me like family. He shared the company's history, regaling me on each visit with stories of his time at the store, his father, and his grandfather."

When the documentary aired in September of 2013 on CBC Radio One, it told the story of not only a suit, but also of fatherhood and of an industry in the throes of change.

Asked about his plans for the business, Terry said that none of his three sons was interested in taking it over and that his only tailor, Alfonso, was nearing retirement, with no one ready to step into his shoes. "Will I be here in ten years?" he mused into the microphone. "I'm not so sure."

It was a question that Terry had been pondering for almost a decade. Early in the 2000s, he was unable make up his mind because his three sons were still in school and hadn't decided what they wanted to do with their lives. Like his father, Terry didn't put pressure on any of his sons to join the business, partially because of his own unease about the industry's future. But his concerns went beyond fluctuating sales and shifting menswear trends. For years,

Terry had attempted to find a tailor to work in Alfonso's shadow, someone who would take over when he retired. But the decades of ready-to-wear and designer clothes had affected more than men's wardrobes; they had also led to the disappearance of the craftspeople who could create them. Although Toronto was still welcoming immigrants from around the world, few brought traditional tailoring skills. Terry feared that the business would not be self-sustaining without a skilled master tailor from the old world.

The tipping point came in April of 2014, when Terry received a reminder from his landlord that the lease at 145 Wellington would soon expire and he would need to renew it for

FACING *Pedro Mendes wearing his Walter Beauchamp Tailors custom three-piece suit in the Wellington Street tailor's studio in November 2013.*

ABOVE *Terry Beauchamp in the measuring room of Beauchamp's Wellington Street store, 2003.*

OVERLEAF *The new home of Walter Beauchamp Tailors inside Holt Renfrew Men at 100 Bloor Street, 2013.*

another ten years. After a span of 106 years, with Terry, his father, and his grandfather having put in equal stints running the store, the time had come to shut the doors permanently. It was not a fraught decision for Terry: by then, his sons had graduated from university and had started satisfying careers in other industries. Without a replacement for Alfonso, Terry knew he could not maintain the level of quality and craftsmanship he had committed himself to. He would have to restock the talent pool. But he, too, was nearing retirement, so perhaps it was time for a new challenge.

Terry even thought long and hard about what his father and grandfather would have said to him on the eve of such a momentous decision. Terry was sure they both would have said that he had made a wise decision and that they were proud of him.

Terry began calling customers to break the news personally. He met with varying degrees of shock and sadness as well as an intense respect for what Beauchamp's had accomplished and an understanding of his decision. He received many calls and notes over that summer of 2014. The following excerpt from a letter written by long-time friend and customer Martin Guest captures the emotions underlying the important relationships that had made the company successful since the days of Terry's grandfather:

The news of your impending retirement caused me to reflect on the years that we have known each other, and I realized that the nature of our relationship is longer, deeper, and more intimate than one might expect. From the day I walked into Adelaide Street, 30 years ago, we've been through a lot together. We've shared graduations and new beginnings, job changes and fresh challenges, weddings and funerals, frustrations and anxieties, weight gains and losses, and so much more. There simply aren't many people who have that kind of viewpoint into another person's life: in your role, you have had an extraordinary proximity and a unique lens on what's going on with me and so many others. It must be fascinating! Of course, none of it would happen without your personal charm, empathy, friendship, insight, kindness, support, and wisdom in matters sartorial and otherwise. For all that I am personally grateful: it's been quite a ride together.

The news of Beauchamp's closing eventually reached the ears of *Globe and Mail* writer Marcus Gee, a high-school friend of Terry's. It was Gee's piece, "A Toronto shop's tailor-made legacy, after 106 years," published on July 4, 2014, that helped usher in a new chapter for Walter Beauchamp Tailors.

Unbeknownst to Terry, a certain senior executive had read Gee's article with deep interest. He was a customer of Beauchamp's, as well as a director of George Weston Limited, and he asked Terry during a fitting whether anyone from Holt Renfrew (a Weston company) had contacted him. No one had, but many other tailors in the city had called, wanting to buy Terry's customer list and stock. Terry had refused all offers. He wanted the Beauchamp name to find a good home or else he would retire it.

A few days later, three executives from Holt Renfrew arrived at Beauchamp's with an unexpected offer. "You have an iconic brand," they told him, "and it's important to the city. We can't just let it fade away." They proposed a partnership—a deal that was very different from the sale that Walter Beauchamp Sr. had made to Samuel Kalles seven decades earlier. It would see Terry license the Beauchamp name to Holt Renfrew, and it would include jobs for the shop's staff, as well as for Terry himself,

who was asked to stay on as a consultant. As the heart and soul of the company, Terry would play a key role in the transition. "And what about military tailoring?" Terry asked during the negotiations. "Holt Renfrew has never done military," Terry was told, but he stuck to his guns, as it were. The Holt Renfrew executives agreed that, to honour the history of the company, Beauchamp's would remain a civil and military tailor.

Terry was mulling over this offer in the summer of 2014 when Holt Renfrew upped the ante. Subject to Terry's approval, the executives offered to earmark a percentage of all Walter Beauchamp sales at Holt Renfrew for the Bruce Beauchamp Memorial Fund. The fund that Terry's family had set up almost three decades earlier would be able to continue its work. At that point, Terry knew that an agreement with Holt Renfrew was the right move. And so, in October of 2014, with a tinge of sadness but a surge of hope, Terry closed the doors at 145 Wellington Street West and opened new ones as part of Holt Renfrew Men at 100 Bloor Street West. Walter Beauchamp Tailors would have an eighth location as it strode boldly into the twenty-first century.

Nowadays, Toronto would be unrecognizable to Walter Sr. When he founded the company in 1908, nearly nine out of ten Torontonians were of British descent. More than half of today's citizens of the city were born outside Canada, and Toronto was recently named the most culturally diverse city in the world. Its population comprises 230 nationalities. And what a population it is. In 2014, the Greater Toronto Area was home to slightly more than six million people; in other words, almost one in five Canadians lives in or around Toronto.

This massive demographic shift is perhaps at the root of the spirit imbuing the city. Gone, finally, is the staid, conservative, puritanical Toronto of years past, replaced by a truly global city. And whether or not Torontonians believe it, the rest of the world does. In a 2012 poll, people in the United States and the United Kingdom deemed Toronto one of the greatest cities in the world. "There's a view, particularly from those in the U.K., that it's a leading city," Mario Canseco, then-vice president of Angus Reid Public Opinion, said. "It's a world-class city for 70 per cent, which is something we didn't quite expect."

But, despite Toronto's sweeping changes, some things stay reassuringly the same. On a sunny Sunday afternoon soon after Walter Beauchamp Tailors moved into Holt Renfrew Men, Terry was standing outside the shop on Bellair Street in the Yorkville district. He was waiting for an associate when he glimpsed a familiar face across the street. It was Charles Ormiston, who had been a customer at Beauchamp's since Walter Jr.'s time (Ormiston's father had shopped there for even longer), although Terry had not seen him in many years. Terry greeted Ormiston warmly and then asked what he was doing in the neighbourhood, recalling that he lived outside the city. "I came into town to pick up some clothing," Ormiston told Terry. And then he asked what was new with Terry, who replied, "We're part of Holt Renfrew now." Ormiston was taken aback but didn't miss a beat: "Well, you know, I need to update my wardrobe. There's just one thing: Can I still get the classic styles and that great Beauchamp service? Can you still do things the way you used to?"

"Of course we can," Terry replied with a big smile. ::

THE G20 SUMMIT

During its nearly thirty years at 145 Wellington Street, the event that had by far the most impact on the day-to-day running of Walter Beauchamp Tailors was the G20 Summit in June of 2010. Against the better judgment of many, the forum that brought together heads of state and central bank governors from twenty of the world's most powerful economies was held at the Metro Toronto Convention Centre in the heart of the city. The central location required a security setup that would swell to become the biggest and most costly in the country's history.

Terry wasn't sure what to expect until he was contacted by the Toronto Police Service a few weeks before the summit. Two officers were going door to door in the neighbourhood, letting businesses know that staff wouldn't be able to access their stores. They warned Terry that his store was inside the security perimeter that would be set up around the convention centre and protected by police, security guards, and a three-metre-high fence. Terry recalls being told, "It's going to be bad; it's going to be ugly." He was advised to prepare for disruptions and even violence.

During the week leading up to the summit, held on June 26 and 27, Terry shut down the store. He gave his staff a week off with pay and he spent thousands of dollars to board up his windows as a preventative measure. Thankfully the summit's violent protests never reached the store, and Beauchamp's survived one of Toronto's darker chapters. Terry received only minor compensation, however, for the costs of shutting down the store and for lost sales. ::

CLOCKWISE FROM TOP LEFT *A view of the barricades on Wellington Street west of Simcoe during the lead-up to the G20 Summit on June 23, 2010; A view from inside Beauchamp's Wellington Street store as members of the Toronto Police Service prepare for the G20 Summit on June 23, 2010; A view of the Wellington Street store through the G20 barricades, June 23, 2010; Terry Beauchamp discussing his preparations for the G20 Summit with customers, June 25, 2010.*

I wish to offer congratulations to Walter Beauchamp Tailors Inc., for 100 years of offering quality products and services to Canadians.

This country was built in large part by entrepreneurs like you who contributed to the economic development of Canada by meeting the needs of Canadians. These businessmen and women helped to set Canada on the path towards achieving success in their individual communities and in the global business world.

On this milestone anniversary, I am pleased to send my very best wishes to the Beauchamp family and to their employees for continued good fortune in business and in life.

Michaëlle Jean

December 2008

THE 100TH ANNIVERSARY

In 2008, Terry Beauchamp had the rare honour of celebrating the 100th anniversary of his family's business. To recognize the achievement, he commissioned Toronto graphic designer Robert Blain to create a new company logo. The store did not have a formal logo until Samuel Kalles took over in 1944 and created a traditional-looking "B&H" design. In 1969, when Walter Jr. bought back the company and renamed it Walter Beauchamp Tailors, he used a simple, elegant typeface for his logo. In contrast, Terry wanted a logo that was classic yet contemporary. The most dramatic addition was the image of a swan resting in a crown (see p. i), a symbol from the coat of arms used by the Beauchamp family in England when it was elevated to the peerage in the thirteenth century as the Earls of Warwick.

Terry received letters of congratulation from many prominent government officials, including Dalton McGuinty, Premier of Ontario; the Right Honourable Michaëlle Jean, Governor General of Canada; and the Right Honourable Stephen Harper, Prime Minister of Canada. The country's oldest custom tailor had entered the history books as one of the few Canadian businesses with such a long lineage. ⫶

ABOVE *Terry Beauchamp received the Queen Elizabeth II Diamond Jubilee Medal in 2012 in honour of his significant contribution to the Canadian tailoring industry and Walter Beauchamp Tailors' reaching its 100th anniversary in 2008.*

FACING *A letter from the Right Honourable Michaëlle Jean, the then Governor General of Canada, recognizing Walter Beauchamp Tailors on its 100th anniversary in 2008.*

This certificate is presented to

Walter Beauchamp Tailors Inc.

*in recognition of your one hundredth anniversary.
It gives me great pleasure to extend to you warmest greetings
and best wishes on this special occasion. My colleagues in the Government of
Canada join with me in recognizing this significant achievement and wish you many
more years of continued success.*

The Rt. Hon. Stephen Harper, P.C., M.P.
Prime Minister of Canada
Ottawa 2008

This certificate is presented to

Beauchamp & How Tailors Inc.

*on the occasion of its 100th anniversary. You may take pride in the century
of hard work and dedication that have made your family business an
enduring enterprise.
On behalf of the Government of Canada, please accept my best wishes for
continued success.*

May 2009

The Rt. Hon. Stephen Harper, P.C., M.P.
Prime Minister of Canada

FACING AND ABOVE *Letters from the Right
Honourable Stephen Harper, the then Prime
Minister of Canada, recognizing Walter Beauchamp
Tailors / Beauchamp & How on its 100th
anniversary in 2008.*

OVERLEAF *A letter from Dalton McGuinty, the then
Premier of Ontario, recognizing Walter Beauchamp
Tailors on its 100th anniversary in 2008.*

Ontario

On behalf of the Government of Ontario,

I am pleased to congratulate the staff and management of

WALTER BEAUCHAMP
TAILORS INC.

on the occasion of this fine organization's 100ᵗʰ anniversary.

The enterprise and the hard work of those who have built

Walter Beauchamp Tailors Inc. over these many decades is an accomplishment

that has benefited the community and our province.

May the years ahead bring further achievement.

Legislative Building, Toronto
December 31, 2008

Dalton McGuinty
Premier

ACKNOWLEDGMENTS

Terry Beauchamp would like to offer heartfelt thanks to his wife Helen and his sons Craig, Scott, and Adam for their constant love and inspiration.

Pedro Mendes would like to thank his wife Marijke Friesen for her support, guidance, and patience through the many, many months of research and writing that turned their lives upside down. And thanks as well to his beautiful son Jonah, who is a daily reminder that there is more to life than dressing up.

And the authors would like to extend their special thanks to the following people who went above and beyond in helping make this book a reality: Neil Brochu and Gabrielle Major at City of Toronto Museums & Heritage Services; Major John Stephens, Master Corporal Graham Humphrey, and Captain (Ret'd) Larry Hicks at the Queen's Own Rifles of Canada Museum; Gregory Loughton, Susan Cook, Bill Hines, and Ryan Goldsworthy at the Royal Canadian Military Institute; Toronto researcher extraordinaire Jamie Bradburn; Terry's lifelong friend, and eagle-eyed editor, Marilyn Thomson; Clifford Weirmeir of the Irish Regiment of Canada; Captain P.J. VanAuken, Director of Music of the Governor General's Horse Guards; Major Scott Duncan, Commanding Officer of the Governor General's Horse Guards; Kathy and Noel Chesher (son and daughter-in-law of Mert); and long-time customers and friends Martin Guest, Bryce Douglas, Judge Donald Dodds, Lionel Goffart, and Charles Ormiston.

NOTES AND SOURCES

Chapter 1 All Walter Beauchamp Sr.'s letters to Viola Mackenzie from the collection of Terry Beauchamp. City growth statistics in Careless (1984). Descriptions of old King Street West from "A Look Back: 'Exciting, Fashionable and Busy,'" the *Toronto Daily Star*, 17 Nov 1962, 34. John Mackenzie's farm from R.B. Fleming audio interview with Viola Beauchamp on 2 Sept 1973. Company incorporation listed in "Many new 'limiteds,' business flourishing," the *Toronto Daily Star*, 24 Oct 1908, 17. R. Score & Son history from Robinson (1885). Ahlgren's information from advertisement in the *Toronto Daily Star*, 11 Oct 1913, 19. "Men's Clothing and Furnishings Department," the *Dry Goods Review*, October 1908, 119–23. Ferris wheel history from Anderson (1992). Baseball scores from "Tecumsehs still on top but must win Saturday," the *Toronto Daily Star*, 22 July 1907, 9.

Chapter 2 Number of dead and wounded in the First World War from Careless (1984). Royal Flying Corps tailoring from "King St. Landmark: 50 Years of Service by Beauchamp and How," the *Globe and Mail*, 28 Sept 1956, 12. Pellatt and Mackenzie's relationship from Fleming (1991). Pellatt's self-funded QOR trip to the United Kingdom from Careless (1984). J.W. Bishop information from http://www.airandspace.si.edu/. History of Royal Flying Corps Canada from Hunt (2009). Transcript of interview conducted with Charles Osborne Dalton in 1998 from Queen's Own Rifles of Canada Museum (https://qormuseum.org/soldiers-of-the-queens-own/dalton-charles-osborne/). Colonel Everett biography from "Horse Guards O.C. Is Named," the *Globe and Mail*, 7 Dec 1937; "Horse Guards Get New C.O," the *Globe and Mail*, 29 Sept 1937; "Governor-General's Horse Guards Embark Today for Camp Training," the *Globe and Mail*, 19 June 1937; "Everett Urges Copy of Swiss Militia Plan," the *Globe and Mail*, 17 Nov 1938; "A.J. Everett Made Colonel," the *Globe and Mail*, 25 Nov 1941; "Belgians Give Decorations to Canadians," the *Globe and Mail*, 4 Nov 1942; "COE. Everett Sent to Coast," the *Globe and Mail*, 7 July 1942. Canadian war-bride information from veterans.gc.ca.

Chapter 3 Beauchamp & How addresses from *The Toronto City Directory* 1918 and 1919, Might Directories Limited. Basement location of tailoring room from interview with Norman Laughlen, son of Charles, Beauchamp tailor in the 1930s. TRC contract details from Filey (1990). Viola Mackenzie streetcar ride from Fleming (1991). TRC's poor relationship with the city from Lemon (1985). Multiple railway lines from Jamie Bradburn article in the *Torontoist*, 17 Sept 2011. Tailors' Association speech from *Men's Wear Review*, January 1931. Hemingway and the Sunday blue laws from Lemon (1985) and Cotter (2004). New athletic male form and the drape cut from Mears and Boyer (2014). R.L. Hewitt quotation from *Men's Wear Merchandising*, 26 Feb 1938. Alf How obituary "Well-known tailor Major A.D. How dies," the *Toronto Daily Star*, 8 July 1940, 9. Alf How funeral details from Hill (2010). Morris Teourliou obituary "Dies while at work," the *Globe and Mail*, 1 Jan 1929, 12. D.W. Harvey testimony from the *Mail and Empire* and the *Globe*, 4 Mar 1930. Judge Denton's findings from the *Toronto Evening Telegram*, 1 Apr 1930 and the *Globe*, 2 Apr 1930.

Chapter 4 Purchase agreement between Kalles Clothing Limited and Walter N. Beauchamp, Viola Beauchamp, and Walter N. Beauchamp Jr., collection of Terry Beauchamp. Death of Frank Score in the *Globe and Mail*, 20 Jan 1947, 5. Score takeover advertisement from the *Globe and Mail*, 11 June 1951, 4. Balaclava overcoat in the *Globe and Mail*, 5 Oct 1960, 4. Toronto's economic and development growth from Lemon (1985). Harold Kalles death announcement in the *Globe and Mail*, 12 Aug 1963.

BIBLIOGRAPHY

"Oldest Firms Adopt Newest Men's Style," the *Globe and Mail*, 28 Feb 1961, 19. "Two Button Suits in Metro Not New, Says Tailor," the *Globe and Mail*, 15 Feb 1966, 11.

Chapter 5 "Merchant Clothiers Follow a Tradition," the *Globe and Mail*, 29 Dec 1977, F1. Growth of Toronto's financial sector, development, and population from Lemon (1985) and Levine (2013). "Edward Dunlop newspaper chief was tough MPP," the *Globe and Mail,* 7 Jan 1981, 11. Announcement of Merton Chesher's decision to join Beauchamp's, the *Globe and Mail,* 26 Sept 1980, B2. Interview with Ken Jones, June 2016.

Chapter 6 "The Economic Impact of SARS," 8 July 2003, http://www.cbc.ca/news2/background/sars/economicimpact.html. Walter Beauchamp radio documentary aired as part of "Men of the Cloth" on CBC Radio One's *Living Out Loud,* 15 Sept 2013. Toronto demographics from Lemon (1985) and Toronto Foundation's 2015 *Toronto's Vital Signs® Report.* Cultural diversity from BBC Radio 4, "More or Less: Behind the Stats," May 2016. "Poll shows Toronto ranks as world-class city in eyes of Americans and Britons," the *Toronto Star,* 16 July 2012. "G8/G20: Gearing up for the biggest security event in Canadian history," the *National Post,* 25 Feb 2010.

Anderson, Norman D. *Ferris Wheels: An Illustrated History.* Madison, WI: Popular Press, 1992.

Breward, Christopher. *The Suit: Form, Function and Style.* London: Reaktion Books, 2016.

Careless, J.M.S. *Toronto to 1918: An Illustrated History.* Toronto: James Lorimer & Company, 1984.

Cotter, Charis. *Toronto Between the Wars.* Richmond Hill, ON: Firefly Books Ltd., 2004.

The Cutter's Practical Guide to British Military Service Uniforms. London: The John Williamson Company Limited, 1913.

Dress Regulations for Officers of the Royal Air Force. London: His Majesty's Stationery Office, 1929.

Filey, Mike. *Not a One Horse Town: 125 Years of Toronto and Its Streetcars.* Willowdale, ON: Firefly Books, 1990.

_____. *The TTC Story: The First Seventy-Five Years.* Toronto: Dundurn Press, 1996.

_____. *Toronto: The Way We Were.* Toronto: Dundurn Press, 2008.

Fleming, R.B. *The Railway King of Canada.* Vancouver: UBC Press, 1991.

Hayes, Derek. *Historical Atlas of Toronto.* Vancouver: Douglas & McIntyre Ltd., 2008.

Hill, Douglas A. *The Families of J. Beverly Fraser and Elizabeth W. How of Toronto, Canada.* Toronto: D.A. Hill, 2010.

Hunt, C.W. *Dancing in the Sky: The Royal Flying Corps in Canada.* Toronto: Dundurn Press, 2009.

Leggatt, W.E., and T.W. Hodgkinson. *The "Climax" System for Cutting Gentlemen's Garments,* 4th ed. London: Minister & Co. Ltd., ca. 1924.

Lemon, James. *Toronto Since 1918.* Toronto: James Lorimer & Co., 1985.

Levine, Allan. *Toronto: Biography of a City.* Vancouver: Douglas & McIntyre Ltd., 2013.

Marteinson, John. *The Governor General's Horse Guards: Second to None.* Toronto: Robin Brass Studio Inc., 2002.

Mears, Patricia, and G. Bruce Boyer. *Elegance in an Age of Crisis: Fashions of the 1930s.* New York: Yale University Press, 2014.

Robinson, C.B. *History of Toronto and County of York, Ontario.* Toronto, 1885.

INDEX

Page numbers for photographs and illustrations are in italics.

CREDITS

P. 38   City of Toronto Museums and Heritage Services, 1968.74.19F.

P. 39   *left and right* Collection of City of Toronto Museums and Heritage Services, 1968.76.23.8. Photos by
           Pedro Mendes, February 2016.

P. 40   *The Cutter's Practical Guide to British Military Service Uniforms* (London: The John Williamson
           Company Limited, 1913). Collection of Terry Beauchamp.

P. 42   Collection of the Queen's Own Rifles of Canada Regimental Museum and Archives, Toronto.
           Photo by Pedro Mendes, March 2016.

P. 43   Collection of the Queen's Own Rifles of Canada Regimental Museum and Archives, Toronto.

P. 44   Collection of the Queen's Own Rifles of Canada Regimental Museum and Archives, Toronto.

P. 45   Collection of Terry Beauchamp.

P. 46   Collection of the Queen's Own Rifles of Canada Regimental Museum and Archives, Toronto.
           Photo by Pedro Mendes, April 2016.

P. 47   Collection of the Queen's Own Rifles of Canada Regimental Museum and Archives, Toronto.
           Photo by Pedro Mendes, April 2016.

P. 48   Photo by Lawrence Cortez, June 2016.

P. 49   Photo by Lawrence Cortez, June 2016.

P. 51   Courtesy of the Governor General's Horse Guards archives.

P. 52   Collection of Terry Beauchamp. Photo by Lawrence Cortez, March 2015.

P. 53   Photo by Lawrence Cortez, March 2015.

P. 54   Collection of Terry Beauchamp.

P. 55   Photo courtesy of the Gibson family.

P. 56   Photo courtesy of the Gibson family.

P. 57   *top and bottom* From the records of Walter Beauchamp Tailors.

P. 59   *left and signature* Collection of Terry Beauchamp.

P. 59   *right* Collection of the Royal Canadian Military Institute, Toronto. Photo by Lawrence Cortez, June 2016.

P. 60   *top* Courtesy of the Department of National Defence, undated.

P. 60   *bottom* Photo by Pedro Mendes, June 2016.

P. 61   Photo TN2009-0237-02, Department of National Defence, by Private Allyssa Carter.

P. 64   City of Toronto Archives, Fonds 1244, Item 536.

P. 65   City of Toronto Archives, *Globe and Mail* Fonds 1266, Item 6724.

P. 66   *all* From W.E. Leggatt and T.W. Hodgkinson's *The "Climax" System for Cutting Gentlemen's Garments,*
           4th edition (London: Minister & Co. Ltd., ca. 1924).

P. 67   From "The History of the Toronto Fire Department," City of Toronto Archives, Fonds 2, Series 1099.

P. 68   Collection of Terry Beauchamp. Photo by Lawrence Cortez, June 2016.

P. 72   Photo originally published in *Men's Wear Merchandising*, February 26, 1938.

P. 73   With permission of the Royal Ontario Museum ©2016 ROM.

P. 75   Collection of Douglas Hill.

P. 76   City of Toronto Archives, Fonds 16, Series 71, Item 12578.

P. 77   City of Toronto Archives, Fonds 16, Series 71, Item 13086.

P. 78   City of Toronto Archives, Fonds 16, Series 323, File 45.

P. 79   *left* City of Toronto Archives, Fonds 16, Series 71, Item 19035.

P. 79   *right* City of Toronto Archives, Fonds 16, Series 71, Item 19036.

P. 82   City of Toronto Archives, Fonds 124, File 1, Item 89.

P. 83   Courtesy of the *Globe and Mail*.

P. 84   Courtesy of the *Globe and Mail*.

P. 85   City of Toronto Archives, Fonds 1231, Item 846.

P. 86   Courtesy of the *Globe and Mail*.

P. 87   City of Toronto Archives, Fonds 1244, Item 10094.

P. 88   Collection of Terry Beauchamp.

P. 90   *all* Courtesy of the *Globe and Mail*.

P. 92   Collection of Terry Beauchamp.

P. 93   Collection of Terry Beauchamp.

P. 94   City of Toronto Archives, Goads Fire Insurance Plans, 1923 (1910), Plate 6.

P. 95   Courtesy of the *Globe and Mail*.

P. 96   Collection of Terry Beauchamp.

P. 97   *top and bottom* Collection of Terry Beauchamp.

P. 98   Courtesy of the *Globe and Mail*.

P. 100   Collection of Eric Liphardt. Photo by Lawrence Cortez, April 2015.

P. 102   Courtesy of the *Globe and Mail*.

P. 104   Courtesy of the *Globe and Mail*.

P. 106   Collection of Terry Beauchamp.

P. 107   Collection of Terry Beauchamp.

P. 110   Collection of Terry Beauchamp.

P. 111   Collection of Bob Kane.

P. 112   Collection of Bob Kane.

P. 113   Collection of Terry Beauchamp. Unknown photographer.

P. 115   Collection of Terry Beauchamp.

P. 116   With permission of the Royal Ontario Museum ©2016 ROM.

P. 117   *left and right* With permission of the Royal Ontario Museum ©2016 ROM.

P. 118   *left* Collection of Noel and Kathy Chesher.

P. 118   *right* Collection of Terry Beauchamp.

P. 119   Ontario Jewish Archives, Fonds 38, Series 8, Item 10.

P. 120   Collection of Bob Kane.

P. 121   Photo by Bob Kane.

P. 122   Collection of Terry Beauchamp.

P. 123   Collection of Terry Beauchamp.

P. 124   *left and right* Collection of Bob Kane.

P. 125   Collection of Terry Beauchamp.

P. 126   Collection of Terry Beauchamp. Unknown photographer.

P. 127   Collection of Terry Beauchamp.

P. 128   Collection of Terry Beauchamp.

P. 129   *top* Collection of Terry Beauchamp.

P. 129   *middle* Photo by Bob Kane.

P. 129   *bottom* Photo by Bob Kane.

P. 131   Photo by Jim Brandenburg/National Geographic Creative.

P. 134   Courtesy of Getty Images.

P. 135   Courtesy of AMC.

P. 138   Photo by Lawrence Cortez, 2013.

P. 139   Photo by Kaleidoscope Photography, 2003.

P. 140   Courtesy of Holt Renfrew, 2014.

P. 142   Courtesy of Getty Images.

P. 145   *all* Collection of Terry Beauchamp.

P. 146   Collection of Terry Beauchamp.

P. 147   Courtesy of the Office of the Governor General of Canada.

P. 148   Collection of Terry Beauchamp.

P. 149   Collection of Terry Beauchamp.

P. 150   Collection of Terry Beauchamp.